A Horse in the Ladies' Room

For Ruth - Best wishes! Mary Lou Fuller

By

Mary Lou Fuller

❖

Cover design and drawings by Jim Dugan

❖

Edited by
Kay Amsden
Professor Emerita, University of New Hampshire

ISBN: 0-9657894-0-3

PUBLISHING
Fitzwilliam, New Hampshire

DEDICATION

This book is dedicated to Enoch Fuller, one of New England's most ardent and colorful innkeepers, who believed strongly that integrity, ingenuity and an old-fashioned work ethic were the only way to go! At the Fitzwilliam Inn he was continually faced with the unexpected behaviour of guests and the ever-present challenge of doing business in a 175 year old building.

An inn provides
rest for the weary,
drink for the thirsty,
and
food for the hungry!

Enoch Fuller

FITZWILLIAM INN

*Showing original wrap-around porch
extending to side entrance of the Inn*

March 1964

We work twenty-four hours a day,
eight days a week!

Enoch Fuller

FOREWORD

Who among us hasn't, at some time, harbored the dream of acquiring a Country Inn and settling into the idyllic life of a Yankee Innkeeper. Fortunately, for most of us, we never follow through and experience the rude awakening that awaits all but the most adventurous and best prepared among us, for this is no "nine to five" job.

Enoch Fuller or "Red", as his many friends called him, was both adventuresome and well prepared. A native New Hampshire man and a 1947 graduate of the University of New Hampshire Hotel School, Enoch had worked as assistant comptroller at New Hampshire's legendary Mount Washington Hotel and went on to broaden his hotel management skills at a number of Massachusetts inns and hotels. Red and Mary Lou returned to New Hampshire to manage the newly refurbished John Hancock Inn and, in 1963, purchased one of New Hampshire's fine old inns - The Fitzwilliam Inn. Three years later, they acquired an old house across the street and remodeled it for their home.

Red Fuller had an incurable love of people and politics, and many a significant campaign gathering was held in the old Inn. He came by these interests naturally, for his father had served New Hampshire for many years as its Secretary of State. In addition, he had that wonderful saving grace, a sense of life's absurdities, and the realization that much that seems daunting in life's experiences has its hilarious side, if you can only see it. Fortunately, Red Fuller kept good notes of some of the amusing unusual characters he and Mary Lou knew. In a labor of love, Mary Lou has captured the essence of their life together, bringing up their two children, Joshua and Amey, and somehow ducking the "slings and arrows" of outrageous fortune that only a true Yankee Innkeeper could fully appreciate. Red's untimely death in 1973, at age 48, necessitated a change in the family's life, but in this loving memoir of the trials and brushes with near disaster that go with managing a 175 year old Inn, Mary Lou Fuller brings these experiences and Red Fuller back to us in a manner that is both a charm and a delight!

Walter Peterson

Anyone can land a plate of food
but it takes a trained server to present a meal.
Enoch Fuller

ACKNOWLEDGEMENTS

Grateful thanks to Kay Amsden for her tireless editorial skills and her faith in this project; most especially her encouragement when the book seemed to be more a dream than a reality.

To my personal Picasso, Jim Dugan, deepest appreciation for his talent and unique creativity that have given life to these pages.

People eat with their eyes.

Enoch Fuller

TABLE OF CONTENTS

INTRODUCTION

Webster defines hospitality as "welcoming, convivial and solicitous towards guests"; an innkeeper is simply described as "one who owns an inn". This description does not do justice to the scope and multitude of tasks, planned and unplanned, that innkeeping actually involves; especially when the guests and frailties of an old building keep getting in the way!

Enoch "Red" Fuller tried to prepare me for what I would face as his apprentice and hostess, first at the John Hancock Inn, followed by ten years in Fitzwilliam. He started off saying, "The usual misconceptions about the hospitality industry are that it looks easy, you get all the food you can eat and it's a lucrative business." Then he continued, "Actually we work twenty-four hours a day, *eight* days a week and any extra revenue goes back into the business". Undaunted, I embraced both the innkeeper and innkeeping.

Red was right. I worked longer and harder than I ever had and was physically and emotionally stretched further than I thought possible. I found my "skills" of *eating* in a restaurant or *staying* in a hotel did not make me an innkeeper. With startling rapidity, I learned-by-doing almost before the innkeeper could tell me what to do.

My training included how to graciously leave my hostessing post in a full dining room to go plunge a toilet, sort through a garbage bucket on a quest stranger than fiction and smile politely as guests departed with more "luggage" than they came in with. I became practiced at dealing with weddings, receptions and brides; large and small.

I was beside the innkeeper when he greeted governors and presidential candidates; I was behind him when he was drenched by an overwrought dishwasher and punched in the nose by an out-of-control bartender. I watched his reaction as the "horse" left the ladies' room.

Over thirty years have passed since our time at the Fitzwilliam Inn but thanks to Red's remarkable notes about the unusual people and events of those days, this story can be told. It is a tribute to family, friends and staff who were with us in the 1960's and it is also a very special salute to the Inn guests; without them there would be no book. I have changed the names in some instances to protect the privacy of those who unwittingly find themselves on these pages.

1

I

IN THE BEGINNING

Red

Enoch Fuller was the name officially recorded on his birth certificate in 1925. By the time he was two, he had sprouted a crop of unruly carrot-colored hair, closely followed by a body's worth of freckles. He was known as "Red" from then on. With age, the hair color toned down to strawberry blonde, the freckles blending to a handsome ruddiness. Shaggy white eyebrows were his most distinctive feature; these pitched and rolled expressively over his blue eyes. Shy and sensitive, only those closest to him realized how difficult smiling and laughing were and that he was more at ease with his bookkeeping ledgers than a roomful of people.

Red, youngest child of Abbie and Enoch Fuller, Sr., was seven years younger than his sister, Virginia. Born in a Nashua, New Hampshire hospital, he spent his early childhood in Greenfield and then moved with his family to Manchester.

At thirteen, a debilitating illness was finally diagnosed as Juvenile Diabetes. His father looked upon the disease as an embarrassment and a sign of weakness. He searched for a "quick fix", ultimately finding a clinic in Pennsylvania run by a "quack" who prescribed daily draughts of vinegar as a cure. Red had a very narrow escape.

As a result, he was admitted to the Joslin Diabetic Center, part of the New England Deaconess Hospital where his case was properly regulated. He was taught to monitor his body and control its "brittle" behavior with a balance of food intake and insulin injections. He measured the serum and injected himself two or three times a day.

His father was in state politics and served New Hampshire as Secretary of State for twenty-eight years. Politics interested Red but he was not outgoing by nature and did not relish the rigors of campaigning. However, he would often accompany his father on trips throughout the state. They normally stayed at one of New Hampshire's resort hotels where the manager was a personal friend of the secretary of state.

Red was always treated to a "back of the house" look at the hotel's operation. He watched the smooth and efficient management of food and other resources and would say later it was like "staging a daily performance with the hotel guests clamoring to pay for a role in the play". His fascination with this industry led him to enter the University of New Hampshire to study Hotel Administration.

Throughout his college years he did his internship at the Mount Washington Hotel in Bretton Woods. His assignments ranged from painting chicken coops to putting on a tuxedo and serving as dance partner for unescorted dowager patrons on Saturday nights.

After earning his degree, Red stayed on at the Mount Washington as assistant comptroller during the summer seasons and traveled to Palm Springs, California in winter where he performed the same general duties at the Desert Inn. When the resort circuit no longer held a challenge, he settled at the Uxbridge Inn in Uxbridge, Massachusetts as manager.

Red left innkeeping to try club management and moved to the Tedesco Country Club in Marblehead. After two years he concluded that having as many bosses as there were club members was not a comfortable situation.

He moved on to the Early American Inns Corporation based in Holyoke. His first assignment was assistant manager of The Yankee Pedlar in that city. When the corporation opened its new and largest motel and restaurant, The Yankee Drummer in Auburn, Red was named manager. It was here on Thanksgiving Day, 1961, that our paths first crossed. At the time neither of us had any thought that I would be more than a casual dining room customer and he the serious and thoroughly professional host.

Mary Lou

I was born in 1929 in Bryn Mawr, Pennsylvania and spent a happy, healthy childhood; I was outgoing and had lots of friends.

4

After high school, I began work in an entry-level position in one of Philadelphia's largest banks. My natural ability with people, hard work and a desire to succeed earned me a coveted promotion to the personnel department. The director designed a career-related program in Industrial Psychology for me and I pursued this at the University of Pennsylvania Evening School.

In 1961, I re-located to Worcester, Massachusetts. My mother had recently returned here following my father's death and I felt my ancestral state was where I wanted to be also. My former employer assisted me in obtaining a position in the personnel department of The Guaranty Bank.

That December, as assistant personnel manager, it was my responsibility to make arrangements for the bank's annual staff Christmas dinner and dance. It was to be held at the new Yankee Drummer. The last time I had been there was on Thanksgiving and I remembered being impressed by the maître d'hotel. He was very attentive and made frequent stops at our table to be sure we were enjoying our holiday meal. My mother had commented on his astonishing white eyebrows and the way he swung his shoulders when he walked.

It was this same individual who greeted me when I called at the Drummer to book the Christmas Party. He was the manager it turned out, not the maître d' at all. Red was easy to work with as I chose the components of the meal and toured the banquet room.

The night of the party Red met me at the door of the Drummer. He was wearing a black tuxedo with plaid cummerbund; his coloring enhanced by the tux. The butterflies began circling in my stomach. The evening was a total success. Red and I celebrated with a nightcap after the last guest had departed.

He called me shortly after Christmas and invited me to dinner at the Drummer. It was a delightful evening and interesting also because I got a look at hospitality from a different perspective. Most of all, I discovered I was falling in love.

We had many such dates. Red seemed relaxed with me and I was intrigued by his serious outlook on everything and found it amazing that someone so obviously introverted had chosen the hospitality industry as a career. He had wonderful stories to tell and could create absolute visual images of people and situations.

Orange Juice

One Sunday I offered to prepare a home-cooked meal at my apartment. Red arranged for his assistant, Roger Dionne, to cover for him for a few hours. He enjoyed his dinner and while I cleaned up he stretched out on the couch in the living room. When it was time for him to leave I shook his shoulder to wake him. He opened his eyes and I knew instantly something was terribly wrong. There was no one "in there". He was blank. Perspiration soaked through his shirt, his face and hands were wet with it. I called his name but his only response was incoherent mumbling. It was as if he could not express the simplest thought.

I knew he was due back at the Drummer in fifteen minutes so I called Roger and explained, "Red fell asleep after dinner and now I think he's running a fever. He's not even lucid!" Roger was sympathetic and asked if I had any orange juice. When I said I did he told me to get Red to drink it. "But," he warned, "don't drown him, he may have forgotten how to swallow."

I hung up the phone, and raced to the kitchen thinking, "Orange juice as an antidote; for what? He might not remember how to swallow; how come?" Roger had seemed pretty matter of fact.

I poured out a glass of juice and returned to the living room where Red was still mumbling. I struggled to get him upright but his dead weight kept forcing me off the couch. Finally I flung my leg over his torso and straddled him. I pulled up his head and brought the glass of juice to his lips. "Swallow," I pleaded. He had not forgotten how.

When the glass was empty I discovered I had splashed his shirt front with juice so I returned to the kitchen for a cloth. As I sponged him off, I was suddenly aware he was grinning at me; a lopsided, drunken grin. He was speaking words that had no association to anything or to each other.

I decided that if one glass of orange juice did this well, two would be better. I went back to the kitchen and, as I was pouring out the second glass, something in the hallway caught my eye. Red was standing there. His legs were wobbly and he still wore the comical grin. While I watched, he emptied his pockets on the telephone stand in the hall. Then to my astonishment, he started to undress, dropping his clothes on the floor where he stood. When he was down to his jockey shorts I stepped into the hall and faced him. "What do you think you're doing? Put your clothes back on. We have to get you to the Drummer." It was not clear in my mind what had actually happened to Red and, although I loved him, I was frightened and wanted him in better hands than mine.

As if I didn't exist, he pulled down his shorts, stepped out of them and headed into the bathroom. Dumbfounded, I went to the telephone to call Roger back when I suddenly heard Red's completely normal voice coming from the bathroom. "If you'll hand me my clothes, I'll explain everything."

I passed the clothes through the door.

He was fully dressed when he emerged. The only reminder of the past thirty minutes were the spots of orange juice on his shirt. His embarrassment was obvious and he sank into a chair. Taking a pen and paper out of his pocket he drew a chart. "I'm a diabetic; a brittle diabetic." He showed me the chart he had drawn. "If my blood sugar drops below this point," his pen traced the danger zones, "I counteract it with food; if it climbs above, I take a shot of insulin. I have to control the balance myself. I took extra insulin before I came up here because I wasn't sure what we were having for dinner and I wanted to feel good. Trying to be 'right' for you must have used up extra energy too. I've never had a reaction come on so fast and I certainly have never done anything like *this* before. God! What *must* you be thinking?" "How much I love you," I replied.

"Will you marry me?" he asked. "The disease isn't so bad when you're used to it." When I said "yes" to his proposal he kissed me and muttered, "It must pay to advertise the merchandise in advance."

I had a momentary thought, "Now I've done it, I'm going to be an innkeeper's keeper."

Red and Mary Lou

We were married in the Chancel of All Saints Episcopal Church in Worcester surrounded by friends and family. We spent our wedding night at the Publick House in Sturbridge and then drove to Virginia Beach, Virginia for five days.

On the long trip, we had plenty of time to talk about our future. Red told me he had always dreamed of owning an inn where "he would make all the decisions, have all the fun and responsibility." He thought my career background, coupled with some training from him, would make me the perfect half of an innkeeping team. I could take on the front of the house and dining room while he handled the more technical and specialized area of food and labor costs and business management.

He said he was cut out to be a country innkeeper rather than a hotel man anyway. He bragged about "the toilet plunging innkeepers" turned out by the UNH Hotel School as compared to the suave front desk-clerk types Cornell produced. I laughed at the thought of innkeepers actually plunging toilets but was prepared to do anything as long as we were together.

When we returned from our honeymoon, Red began poring over hotel trade papers and making telephone calls to let the strong "back-of-the-house" network system carry the message that Enoch Fuller was searching for a place to lease or purchase.

Months passed and, as time allowed, we visited a cross section of old hotels and inns in New Hampshire. I learned a lot about my husband's native state and loved all I saw. I found the search process fascinating and was impressed with Red's thorough investigation of each facility we considered.

In October the call finally came that Red was hoping for. Red was thrown into a dither when I told him, "A Mr. John King would like to speak to you." I didn't know that John King was also the name of New Hampshire's current governor.

Our Mr. King turned out to be an interior designer specializing in inns and restaurants. He had recently purchased and restored the John Hancock Inn in Hancock, New Hampshire. He wanted Red to come up and take a look. A date was set and Red was exhilarated when he hung up. He remembered the Hancock Inn as one of the oldest in the state. Mr. King had restored the entire place and planned to re-open in time for the Christmas party season and winter skiing. "He wants to interview us as a manager-hostess team. But the best news is that he plans to keep the inn for only six months and then sell it. Sounds perfect."

Red and Mary Lou

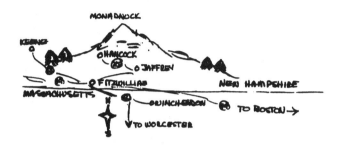

II
ROYAL BLOOD

The Interview

The sign outside read "The John Hancock Inn - Board, Bottle and Bed Since 1789". It was a wonderful old building that rambled back from a wooden porch. The windows on either side of the front door opened onto the porch. Those to the right were tightly shuttered. This secluded the inn's new bar and conformed with New Hampshire law which prohibited windows of any establishment selling "spirituous liquors" from opening onto a public thoroughfare. The intent being to protect innocents who might look in and be corrupted by the sights and sounds of their fellow citizens sloshing about in demon rum.

It was into this dark room that Red and I were ushered for our meeting with John and Jean King. We were introduced to the Kings by the bartender-host and joined them in a booth.

John King was short and square with cat-like features and a grin which never left his face. His ears were large only adding to his feline resemblance. He fingered a handful of nuts and bolts which came and went from a pocket whenever he had something to say. His voice was unusually high: it would have been hard to tell if it was male or female if one was not in his presence.

9

Even sitting down Jean King was six inches taller than her husband. She wore heavy makeup and a look of surprise; no doubt brought on by the exaggerated plucking of her eyebrows.

As I grew accustomed to the dimness, I was able to see more of the room. What I had thought was a booth was in reality a pair of old wagon seats, restored and reupholstered; a gigantic blacksmith bellows had been split in half with legs added to make the table. Directly opposite was a massive bar with six black leather stools. A wrought iron horse stall divider stood at one end giving the illusion of a private drinking area. The fire flickering in the hearth provided the only light.

John jumped up and bounded off gesturing for Red to follow. I was left with Jean. We sat in silence for a minute or two and suddenly, in a careful voice she began a litany of the items on their menu ending with the comment, "John and I want this to be a gourmet dining room featuring foods from around the world. We like exotic dishes. We'll drive miles to find a restaurant that serves Hearts of Palm or Grape Leaves." I could not think of a reply; I assumed a New England inn featured New England dishes. Presently she thought of more to say, "I like the bath towels folded in threes and the napkins in fours. If there is a special party, the napkins are to be folded in fans or peaks." I was about to ask how one differentiated between parties that warranted fans or peaks, when Red and John reappeared.

Red beckoned me to step outside. "He wants to hire us right away. Hardly asked me any questions but seemed to know all the details of my background." He looked up at the building and continued, "This place only has twelve guest rooms and six baths. He's made the bar so damned big there's no place for house guests to sit and read or play cards. We'd have to do everything ourselves except cook and wait on table. I'd have to learn bartending. I just don't know if I'd be happy in such a small place."

I felt he wanted my encouragement and support so I replied lightly, "What the 'book' says you do in a large place, you just chop in half for one this size, right? If you think you can shrink the book to fit, let's do it." Red went on as if I hadn't spoken and I knew his mind was made up. "He won't pay much but it's possible this will work into the lease or purchase we want. It's a nice town and not far from our mothers. We'll make friends. I'll tell him we'll take it."

We returned to Massachusetts and gave the required notice at our respective jobs.

The Move
Although Red knew nothing about driving a large vehicle, we rented a

The John Hancock Inn

U-Haul truck. As he turned corners we careened over curbs narrowly missing light poles and pedestrians. It was a wild ride until he got the "beast" under control. Then, after packing and loading the truck, we headed immediately for New Hampshire.

The apartment assigned to us at the Hancock Inn consisted of two rooms; a bedroom and living room. The rooms were built into the front end of the second floor warehouse over the kitchen. The bath was set apart from our rooms because it was shared by the staff and was centrally located near the top of the back stairway. I could see my breath in the apartment and asked Red about the heat. "No radiators?" Although he was bone weary, he went downstairs to look for Mr. King and ask about the heat and someone to help unload the truck.

He was distraught when he returned. "He expected us to work tonight so he wouldn't have to keep the bartender on. He forgot about hooking up the radiators and there's no one to help us with the furniture until tomorrow. He told me to take one of the guest rooms for a few nights." I covered my disappointment because I could see how discouraged Red was. He must have felt he had really lost face in front of his bride. We had been so enthusiastic when we left that morning, but circumstances and John King had worked against us.

Earle
We went down to the kitchen to find something to eat and Red introduced me to the chef, Earle Aaskov. He was about fifty, medium build,

11

iron-grey hair. He had a wide smile that lighted his face and made his eyes sparkle. His hands were large; long fingers with broad flat nails. Later, when I mentioned his enormous hands to Red he said, "I'll bet he can get six more slices from a quarter inch piece of onion with hands like that. They're almost a trademark in his line of work."

Earle was quite handicapped and I found this unusual for someone whose chosen vocation required him to be on his feet constantly. He wore a big shoe on his left foot and that leg was permanently bent causing him to walk with a rolling gait that pitched his body forward with each step. In order to keep his balance when he was standing still, he anchored himself by parking the toe of the big shoe in a vertical position against the floor. This wonderful man was to become a friend and mentor and would play an important role in our lives for the next nine years.

Earle told us that Mr. King had gone home leaving Chris, the bartender, in charge. The dining room was quiet so the chef gave us each a bowl of his delectable vegetable soup and sat down with us as we ate. He had to sit with the crippled hip off the seat of the chair to accommodate his inability to change its position. He told us about himself and his background. "Aaskov is Danish, in case you wondered," he began. "I started out as a builder and was doing O.K. until I fell from a ladder and smashed my left hip. Without good insurance I couldn't afford the surgery to fix it right. With the building trade off-limits to me, I hired out to Valle's Steak House when they opened their new place in Scarborough, Maine. I did everything at Valle's. Every damned job no one else would do including washing pots and swill buckets. They do a lot of broiling there and I learned to be a good broiler man."

He went on to tell us that he moved from one restaurant to another picking up new skills and perfecting the old until he became proficient in all levels of food preparation from soups to roasts, sauces, Newburgs and even baking. I thought he must have built up an excellent reputation for John King to have hired him for his "jewel" of Hancock, and said so.

Earle described the rest of the kitchen staff which included a full-time baker-breakfast cook, Ruth Higgins, from Hancock and an elderly man who did the dishes. "By hand!" Earle exclaimed. Like our radiators, "The King", as Earl called him, had not gotten around to hooking up the dish machine.

Red had told me some horror stories about chefs and their temper tantrums. He knew owners and managers who did not dare set foot in their own kitchens because of the sacrosanct atmosphere created by the man in the tall white hat. He said, "Chefs can make or break the food cost by ignoring portion controls which result in over-buying and spoilage. They can make under the table deals with purveyors willing to pad invoices and split the difference with the chef. They can steal your food outright."

However Red doubted Earle was a prima donna. "The most sure-fire way to prevent a chef from taking over," he said, "is an incentive plan or percentage to be paid if the food cost stays where it should each month."

The Environment

Gradually we moved in and got settled. Our apartment rooms were on the front corner of the inn over the bar, with windows facing east and south, giving us a view of the main route in and out of Hancock.

John King was well respected in the field of interior design. He had created the decor in Boston's famous Pier IV Restaurant for Anthony Athanas. But, like many people who make their living providing service to the food industry and are in and out of fine establishments, he thought that somehow through osmosis he had picked up all he needed to know about owning a restaurant. Because he knew what he liked to eat, he thought he could develop a menu. Probably the most difficult sort of boss that a professional like Red could have chosen. On the surface, Red had been hired for his expertise but what he did not know was that John King had also picked up the notion that no one who worked in the food industry was to be trusted, starting with his new manager.

The atmosphere and physical plant of the small inn were a joy to work in. King had decorated it handsomely with a carpet of horse blanket plaid that ran through the entire first floor and up the stairs.

On the left just past the bar, was an intimate dining room with only two tables, each set for eight. The simplicity of the room's decor served to highlight the nine gold stars above the mantlepiece. Positioned there in the earlier days of the inn, they honored New Hampshire as the ninth state to ratify the constitution.

The main dining room ran the full width of the building. Brass pineapple wall sconces gave the room a warm light and, in the evening, there were candles on the tables.

Red was the bartender unless we had a sizable banquet. Then he would have Chris come in to free him to assist with the dining room supervision and help out wherever needed. At first he was slow in mixing drinks and spent a lot of time with his nose buried in *Old Mr. Boston*. The cocktails he made were excellent; he never believed in "free pouring" and carefully measured all ingredients.

There was a telephone extension at the bar and one in the front office. We had our own personal line installed upstairs much to John King's dismay. We were sure he pictured us wasting his time and money talking on the phone.

We worked long hours. Particularly Red who, in addition to the bar duties, ordered all the food and supplies and made trips to the liquor store and bank in Peterborough. Each month he took complete inventories and kept on top of the critical food, beverage and labor costs. He recorded all sales and expenses and could account for everything for which he felt responsible as manager.

With Red's help I had learned hostessing, taking bar orders and scheduling waitresses. I also did most of the housekeeping in the guest rooms. A French woman from Bennington, Noela DuGuay, came in on weekends.

It was a cold and snowy winter but business seemed steady as the holiday season approached. Red was a drawing card, too. He was from the area, his father was well-known and his mother had been born and raised in nearby Greenfield; many folks from that town came to the inn.

The Kings

John and Jean arrived every weekend, often with guests. We had become aware that Mr. King was a naturally suspicious person, but we knew he was getting his money's worth out of Earle Aaskov and the Fullers.

We were shocked when he confronted us in the kitchen one Sunday afternoon. "Fulla," he shouted, "there were two dozen double lamb chops in the walk-in box last Sunday, now there are only ten chops. Where are the rest?" Earle explained with some sarcasm that they had been sold. King demanded to see the dining room checks and, perched on a bar stool, carefully tracked all the orders of double lamb chops sold since his last count. All of this took place with guests in the dining room and bar. When the outcome agreed with the number of remaining chops, he begrudgingly acknowledged that Earle was right, but offered no apology for his unfounded suspicions.

The next Saturday night, just as the dining room was about to open, King made a surprise entrance through the back kitchen door. "I want to check the food," he said. "Beans!" King screamed. "Why do you have beans on my menu? No good place ever serves baked beans on a Saturday night. Why don't you have Hearts of Palm? Get some the next time Fulla orders. Get some! Get some!" Needless to say, Red ordered the Hearts of Palm and had them on the menu the following week. King was frustrated but far from remorseful when not one order was sold

In addition to his surprise visits, King would telephone, most often during a meal hour. We decided he did this purposely to see if we were at our posts. Red would be forced to answer the phone from behind the bar. He had gotten into the habit of tucking the receiver under his chin in order to talk and mix drinks at the same time. One particular day John called and Red, receiver in place, talked as he filled a bar order. He turned quickly to reach for a liquor bottle on the shelf behind him and the receiver, stretched beyond the cord's limit, snapped away from his chin and plunged into the soapy water in the bar sink. Red made a leap for the phone. As it rose from the water, John King's hysterical voice could be heard exploding from the ear piece.

"Fulla! Fulla! Sounds like you're under water out there. What the hell's going on? I better come right out." I was gasping with laughter; but Red, ever the pro, managed to convince "The King" that his inn was not about to float away. Anything to avert a personal visit.

Jean King was no less suspicious of us than her husband and our first indication came in the form of instruction in the art of taking a liquor inventory.

"Now, Mr. Fuller," she began, "you take a liquor inventory in the following manner." Red's patience was remarkable considering that he had been taking inventories of all types during his lengthy career in hotel management. But this was obviously something new for Jean and she was determined to let Red know that she was no dummy.

"You are to save all the empty liquor bottles," she continued, "then at the end of the month, count up each type and divide that number by the total drinks sold according to your daily bar slips." Red couldn't contain himself. "Mrs. King, this will *not* give you an inventory figure, but it *will* tell you if the bartender is stealing." Red told me this procedure was an old one used by many managers who suspected their bartenders were not working for the "house". He was disillusioned to think the Kings considered that he took so little pride in doing a good job.

We always knew when Jean had eaten at a new restaurant. "I don't like the way you are folding these napkins. They should be standing up between the knife and fork, not lying flat like you have them," she would say. Even though "lying flat" was what she had decreed the week before, the napkins would all have to be refolded before any guests could be seated in the dining room.

New Year's Eve

During the four months we were in Hancock, New Year's Eve loomed as the most outstanding. Every table was reserved for dinner and we had set up the banquet room for large parties. It was eight p.m.; the dining room almost full. The staff was going all-out but, with Earle and Red's preplanning, things were running smoothly.

Then the Kings arrived with another couple and no reservation. "We thought you'd know we would be over tonight, Fulla." In his favor, I noticed his face reddened when he looked at the crowded dining room and the business we were doing. Jean, however, demanded to be seated immediately.

Their entrance was the focal point of all activity and people at other tables could not help noticing. This combined with the non- Hancock, flashy cocktail dresses Jean and her friend were wearing and their severe make-up, provided entertainment our guests had not bargained for. "John, pass me the bread basket," Mrs. King was heard to say. He extended the basket across the table and in so doing came too close to the lighted candle. The paper napkin covering the breads burst into flames. "Fire!" she screamed and dropped the basket to the floor. The gentleman with them jumped up and smothered the flames with his linen napkin. There was no real harm done except to Jean's dignity and to cover this, she turned in her chair and bowed from the waist nodding regally to all.

When their dinners arrived, King ordered a bottle of red wine. Red strode to their table and, with a flourish, draped a bar towel over one bent forearm as he approached. He displayed the bottle label and leaned over to pour a small amount into King's glass for his approval. At that exact moment, Jean decided to visit the powder room. As she stood, her shoulder nudged Red's arm and the wine that was intended for John's glass splashed onto her dress; the stain created an amazing Rorschach pattern. I fled to the sanctuary of the kitchen. "They weren't too mad," Red told me later, "just said I'd do better after more practice."

Red was summoned to the kitchen about eleven o'clock. The Kings had left for home; other guests had retired to the bar to wait for midnight. When he got to the kitchen, the dishwasher was waiting for him, apron in hand. "None but a hoss would do all them dishes by hand and I ain't no hoss!" He turned on his heel and walked out the back door.

Red dragged back to the bar. "The dishwasher quit. I told King this would happen if he didn't get that damned machine hooked up. God! You should see the dishes out there." The way he looked at me I knew there was only one move to make. "I'll start them but don't forget where I am at midnight. I want that glass of champagne you promised me."

Neither of us envisioned spending our first New Year's eve wearing long white aprons and washing stacks of dirty dishes. At midnight we toasted each other, the marriage and the Fuller innkeeping team that had survived a grueling test. We washed down peanut butter sandwiches with the champagne.

Jimmy Martin

After New Year's, business slowed down and Ruth Higgins' son or daughter would help out with the dishes. But we needed a full-time person. In addition to the dishes there were some heavy cleaning chores, shoveling and maintenance tasks that were always cropping up.

So, when Jimmy Martin showed up at the kitchen door looking for just such a job, Red hired him. "There's something mysterious about the guy," he explained, "but he needs work as much as we need him. Says he left Boston because blacks are treated so badly there. He'll certainly be left alone here: he's a phenomenon in this area. But he and Earle will get along. I told him he could have the attic room." Shiny black, thin and wiry Jimmy must have been about thirty-five. He was always neatly dressed in the rental uniforms we provided.

Jimmy was a great asset to the place. Even John King agreed that we had made a good choice and had the dish machine connected. Jimmy's room and board was the main part of his salary. He received a small check in addition.

Each evening after the close of business he would leave the kitchen spotless. Then he would sit at the chef's bench, light a candle and perform a ceremony that involved a mantra in words known only to him. If anyone happened into the kitchen during this time he would continue his chanting seemingly lost in a trance. Once it was over, he would snuff the candle, put it in his pocket and go up to his room. Jimmy was good company, he laughed easily, Earle liked him and he would do anything to please. It was worth the curiosity we all had about his nightly seance to have him in our midst.

Last Days at Hancock

John King's temper shortened as the winter lengthened. Snow was piled everywhere with a new storm arriving almost weekly, but the skiers he thought would flock to the inn never came. Business was not as good as he had envisioned.

On many occasions Red had tried to convince him to change to a more reasonable menu; something skiers could afford. John was neither skier nor innkeeper so the foreign dishes, costly and unappealing, stayed put. "He should get away from those Boston prices until winter is over and a different clientele is out on the roads," Red and Earle would say. "Skiers want stews, chowders and other hearty food. You can't go far on Hearts of Palm when you're trying to feed a family that's been out exercising all day." Red also suggested advertising special package deals to go along with the new Crotched Mountain Ski Area; but still King resisted.

Red came to the decision that the time was right to make an offer to purchase the Hancock Inn. He took into consideration the slow times and John King's uncertainty about the business in general. Perhaps King was ready to unload it and save face before he went "under".

We had talked over the financial undertaking more than once and Red, in his methodical, careful way, had spent many a late night factoring in all the known's and maybe's that could influence the industry. He also said, "We won't have our own salaries to pay; just Earle, Jimmy and a few waitresses. We're already doing double duty; might as well do it for ourselves."

I was pleased. I liked Hancock and the townspeople we had gotten to know. It was principally a retirement town but there were also younger couples with whom we had become quite friendly. These very friends were the ones who told us that John King had paid only $12,000 for the inn.

"It's true he's made a lot of improvements," Red reasoned. "I'll probably insult him with my offer, but I think $25,000 is a fair price for the business this place will generate; I'll back it up with an operating statement and projections."

Insult was an understatement. John King ranted on and on the night Red presented his offer. He strode up and down in the bar, fingering his nuts and bolts and turning a deep red. In the end he pounded the wall with his fist and screamed, "$75,000 is my price for Hancock. Don't you know I've got $50,000 of my blood in this place? Blood, do you hear me?" "Mr. King,"

Red replied calmly, "the last thing Mary Lou and I would *ever* want is any of *your* blood."

That evening just about finished us with John King. There was no bargaining with him, he refused to negotiate and finally told us in no uncertain terms that he would never sell us the Hancock Inn at any price.

It was not long after this that prospective management teams began appearing with the Kings. Although our situation was precarious, we could not help but chuckle when we heard the same line about "foreign dishes and selling or leasing within six months" creep into the conversation.

We decided that this time our move would be to our own place; lease or purchase. Red talked with purveyors who came by regularly, and told them we were in the market for an inn or small hotel in New Hampshire. Once again the back-of-the-house network was set in motion.

On an especially warm evening in March, when the mixture of air against lingering snow created a considerable fog, Red and I were sitting alone in the bar. It was almost eight o'clock and we were about to close early when the front door opened and an older couple entered.

When they had been seated in the dining room, Red said to me, "I think they're the Bicknells from the Fitzwilliam Inn." "Where's that?" I wanted to know. "Twenty-five miles south of here. I've never been there, but I've heard a lot of good things about it. It's right on the Massachusetts state line and an easy draw from the Boston area. The Inn was always a summer place until Bicknell came along. He built a ski tow nearby and has been able to keep the Inn open in winter. Funny they should be way over here on a night like this. I'm going out to see Earle, let me know when they're finished."

Red reappeared. "That *is* the Bicknells. Earle looked through the kitchen door and feels sure about it. Let's get them to come into the bar for an after-dinner drink," Red suggested. I went over to their table, introduced myself and extended our invitation.

As it turned out, Mr. Bicknell had nothing to drink and Phyllis downed hers so fast Red decided not to offer her any more. It was difficult for me to concentrate on the conversation with Phyllis muttering comments each time her husband spoke. Suddenly Mr. Bicknell was standing up, saying, "Good, we'll see you Thursday. Come for dinner, any time before eight; we close early over there." I had obviously missed some of what transpired between the two men but when we got upstairs, Red told me about it.

"He wants to sell Fitzwilliam. He heard about us and wants us to come over and see the place. It's much too expensive because he's got a swimming pool and sauna bath in addition to the ski tow. We'd never be able to afford it; but he wouldn't talk money. Wants us to see it first."

When Thursday evening arrived, the fog was still a problem and neither of us really wanted to make the fifty mile round trip. But Red had arranged for the waitresses to watch the bar and Earle could cover for us if John King showed up. Anyway, needing a night out, we headed for Fitzwilliam.

As it turned out, this was the most important evening of our lives.

Red by Fitzwilliam Common
with one of old fashioned cars in group
staying at the Inn
(Note the Innkeeper's Key tie clasp)

III
MUSICAL CHAIRS

Fitzwilliam

My first look at the Fitzwilliam Inn was through the March fog as we drove up Route 119 into town. We had to stop at the intersection to get our bearings and suddenly the mist lifted and there it was. I could see the front of the building with its peaked roof and tall brick chimneys. There was an upstairs porch, supported by four pillars that ascended from below. These were a part of the wide veranda that wrapped around the front and side of the Inn.

Red pulled the car up on Richmond Road. I looked up at the building as I got out of the car and was amazed at the size. There were seven chimneys in all. Rows of windows ranged in patterns from the third floor to the first.

As we headed up the brick path, I saw a small wooden sign atop a pipe attached to the porch rail: "An Inn Since 1796". Large granite steps led up to the door. The risers were of varying heights, off by an inch or two making it an awkward climb.

As we entered the door, the atmosphere of the Inn's interior surrounded us with its warmth. It was shabby in comparison with the Hancock Inn, but it had innate grandeur that no amount of decorating could possibly enhance. The carpet runners were bright red, exposing wide floor boards.

We continued up the hall and were greeted by Al and Phyllis Bicknell. We hung our coats and followed our hosts up a stretch of hallway that slanted upward, suddenly catching me off balance. Al laughed and said, "You'd slant too if you were almost two hundred years old!"

He took us into the Pub where I was aware of an aroma: a mixture of good liquor and lingering wood smoke. We were seated at a round table in front of a handsome fireplace. The hearthstone was granite, the mantle a single piece of gleaming wood; the brick chimney exposed to the ceiling. Cranes were hung with cook pots and a black iron oven door was built into the side of the fireplace. This was where all the cooking and baking was done at one time.

The walls in the Pub appeared to be covered with old liquor bottle labels, but on closer inspection I could see it was wallpaper, colorful and entertaining.

Al explained the Pub had been his creation. Once the state began issuing hotel liquor licenses, a separate drinking room was allowed. New Hampshire rules were still very stringent and the only legal position for drinking was sitting down.

Al

I was intrigued by Al Bicknell. He was an English gentleman and spoke with the remnants of an accent. Slightly built and balding but rigidly erect to belie his eighty plus years. I asked how he had come to Fitzwilliam. I knew they had owned the Inn for only five years and was naturally curious about what had attracted him to this little town. He was frank to say he was a millionaire several times over having made his fortune blowing glass laboratory equipment and patenting his designs. He had had several businesses, the most recent MacAllister Bicknell, which produced and sold the equipment to labs and hospitals.

He came to Fitzwilliam purposely because he was intrigued by the name which harked back to the days of George III who was on the throne during the American Revolution. Wentworth, royal governor of New Hampshire, named the town after the family into which he would eventually marry. Al said, "It's the only town in North America so named. If you mail a letter and forget to put on 'New Hampshire', the addressee will still get it!"

After he bought the Inn in the late 1950's, he and Phyllis were married. A short time later he had a ski slope built just up the road; followed by a swimming pool and bathhouse-sauna combination behind the Inn.

The Fitzwilliam Ski Area opened the following winter and not only boosted the Inn business, enabling a year round operation, it also provided employment for local people who ran tows and lifts, served on the ski patrol and operated the snack bar in the base hut.

In the summer he hired a lifeguard and invited the town's people to share the swimming pool along with his house guests. The clay tennis courts that had once occupied the space taken by the pool had been removed and trucked across the street to land that was part of the Inn property. Al explained, "At one time an early hotel had stood there. The four granite blocks that supported the front columns are the only remaining landmark. The leach field for our Inn septic system is over there, too." Little did we realize how this leach field would intrude on our lives.

After two rounds of cocktails, we adjourned to the dining room. My attention was instantly drawn to the four front windows. Small shelves were mounted on the wall between each. The shelves were uniquely crafted to give a scroll-like appearance and displayed colorful dishes. There was a table for two at each window. The ceiling had the original open beams, hand hewn. On the north side of the dining room were two windows, between these another table for two. Throughout the rest of the room were ten tables, well-placed for seating and serving convenience. A new fireplace had been built since the original construction of the building. This backed up to the Pub, sharing the same chimney.

When we were seated, Phyllis leaned over and jabbed me in the ribs with her finger. She squinted one eye shut and pointed at the walls. "What's the matter with the paper?" she asked. Both Red and I examined the wall closest to us and, seeing nothing apparent, said so. "It's on upside down," she chortled. "The woman who cooks breakfast and does the baking put it up. When the job was half done she discovered it, so we had to do the whole room that way. Even the matching curtains are upside down."

Our dinner was plain fare, well prepared and presented. Al told us his chef had quit and a most amazing young local fellow was doing the cooking. "Bob Berry, is the lad's name. He's been able to pick up enough to get us through. I haven't been able to find anything he can't do. His willingness is worth everything in a business like this." Red and I glanced at each other as we knew that if this turned out to be our place, Earle and Jimmy would come with us from Hancock.

We commented about the amount of work that had to go into an inn this size. Al replied, "There's much that's not done. I pay the bills and do a little bartending. Mostly I sit and enjoy the guests, that's why I designed our logo to show the innkeeper and his guest. Shuffleboard and the pool in summer. Phyllis does everything; I love to watch her work, don't I, Lovey?"

After dinner Al and Phyllis took us on a complete tour of the rest of the building and grounds.

The Tour
We started in the front parlour. This was a prime example of an early formal sitting room. The walls were pink with a white border in which classic black stencilling traveled across the top, down the sides and over the wainscotting. Al told us the original stencil had been in the old inn across the street. Before that building was condemned and torn down in the early 1950's, the town corporation, which owned the Inn at that time, commissioned Harrie "Hal" Sherman, a summer resident and interior designer, to make a copy of the original and reproduce it in this room. The carpet was a pink Oriental. However the crowning touch, in my opinion, were the window curtains. These had been a gift from an Inn guest. They were unbleached muslin with an exquisite border of hand-knotted and twisted fringe at least twelve inches deep.

We crossed the hall into the library. It was lined with books and furnished with comfortable couches and chairs. The wainscotting was painted a Colonial red, a braided rug was centered on another wide board floor. Over the fireplace was lettered an Olde English Rebus:

IF THE B m t, PUT:
IF THE B. PUTTING:
DON'T PUT : OVER A -DER
YOU'D BE AN * IT!

Al urged me to decipher it. I tried, knowing full well there was a trick. "If the capital B period, put colon," I began. I saw the corners of Al's mouth begin to twitch. I continued, "Don't put colon over a dashder, you'd be a star it." Al threw back his head and laughed delightedly and quickly recited the correct version:

"If the grate be empty, put coal on
If the grate be full, stop putting coal on
Don't put coal on over a high fender
You'd be an ass to risk it!"

It was my turn to laugh; Red's too. "The story goes," Al explained, "in earlier days coal was burned in a grate set into the fireplace; a brass fender was placed outside the hearth to reflect the heat into the room. A guest wrote the first two lines in chalk on this chimney above the smoldering coals. These two lines remained through several innkeepers. Suddenly one day the last two lines appeared; author unknown." The intriguing Rebus was a drawing card, a source of amusement for innkeeper and guests alike and Al featured it on the Inn postcards.

Across the side entrance hall where Red and I had first entered, was the office where house guests checked in. The front desk itself was a magnificent old piece that had been a part of the Inn for decades. Al pointed to the guest register. It must have been a yard square; at the top an ornate silver tray once held ink wells, pens and pen points. This marvelous relic was attached to the desk and could be swiveled around to facilitate the registering process. There was also a Private Branch Exchange or PBX behind the desk. My face must have shown my surprise because Al said, "All the rooms have phones. Quite a modern convenience, don't you think?"

There was a ladies' room in the corner and, as we exited the office by yet another very narrow and slanting hallway, the men's room was immediately on our left.

Re-entering the dining room we continued to what Al called the back dining room. "Years ago," he said, "this was a wash room; the eating area ended there," as he gestured to the main dining room we had just come through. "All the table linen and dishes were washed here by hand. This entire building was separate at one time."

Al took us into the big old kitchen. It was functional; looked like it would be good to work in. Down two steps in the back was a storeroom with two freezers and an ice machine. Al told us the kitchen and store room were part of yet a third building also connected long ago. Behind the range and ovens we stepped down into a large room duplicating in size, and backing up to, the storeroom. A flight of stairs led up from here and our tour continued to the second floor.

We came into the manager's apartment which was really one large bed-sitting room that looked out over the parking lot. This was where the Bicknells lived. Al had a small office and there was a small storage room. A good-sized bath completed the apartment.

A door at the end of the apartment hall led into the second floor level of the Inn. We continued along, viewing a collection of rooms and baths. As we went it was easy to see where the buildings had been joined together. Hallways tipped and slanted in surprising places. "Like a fun house," I whispered to Red. A steep and narrow flight of steps descended from this back hall. The three doors at the bottom gave one a choice of entering the kitchen, the patio or the back dining room.

The guest rooms on the north side of the second floor rear shared a public bath and shower room; those on the south side had private baths. The rooms at the front of the second floor also had private baths; the two largest commanded a view of the town common and each had a fireplace and television.

A short hallway around the corner from these accommodations led to the third floor stairs which we ascended to see yet another ten rooms. The most impressive was on the very front which again looked out on the center of town. Phyllis took me over to the far right-hand window and squatted down pulling me with her. She pointed out into the dark and fog saying, "When the leaves are off the trees you can see Mt. Monadnock from right here." Like all residents of the Monadnock region, I had quickly become a devotee of this famous landmark. Still I could not avoid a chuckle at the thought of squatting here from November to April to see it.

The Sale

Al asked Red if he would like to see the sauna bath. Phyllis plodded off, saying she would get the room unlocked, thus prompting Al to speak candidly without fear of her overhearing.

As we made our way down from the third floor, he told us more about his reasons for selling the Inn and ski area. "Phyllis has gotten to the point with her drinking where she can no longer cope with all that's required by this business. She insists on doing everything herself and is really unable to do any of it right. Guests are beginning to notice and the staff covers for her all the time. Most critical is our liquor license which the state would revoke if they caught her mixing or serving drinks in this condition. She's dead set against my selling the place and really doesn't believe I'll go through with it; but I've resolved that I must. I'm sitting in a mess and no one realizes but me just how bad it's getting."

Red took this opportunity to interject that he knew nothing about running a ski area. "I realize the Inn can't survive in winter without skiing but it's not what I feel I could do well." Al replied that he would be willing to retain ownership of the ski slope and bring in a manager. He continued, "I'll make it easy financially for you to have the Inn, just say you'll take it and I'll have the papers drawn up." I knew Red was too conservative to move that fast so I was not surprised when he asked to see some figures, have more detail on price and payment arrangements. Al agreed to an appointment to discuss all the particulars.

The Sauna

We collected our coats and proceeded out the back door, along the side of the swimming pool to the bathhouse. The sauna was a small self-contained chamber; in one corner a pile of yellow stones was being heated by the gas stove Phyllis had lighted. The room was filled with hot dry air, making it unbearably suffocating. Al told us the sauna is the Finnish version of a steam bath. "They sit in here naked; not in overcoats." He looked at me and grinned.

Not wanting to show his discomfort or appear rude, Red endured the heat until the lenses in his eyeglasses were opaque. We withdrew as gracefully as we could, thanked the Bicknells and departed for Hancock.

The Deal

During Red's drive back from Fitzwilliam after the meeting with Al, his excitement had accelerated to such heights that he could barely share his news. "Al told me he likes to find talented and deserving young people on whom he can bestow the gift of potential success in their chosen careers. Believe it or not, he had traced my background all the way to my days at UNH and Bretton Woods. He knows I'm not able to purchase anything without a big mortgage and has offered to lease the business and apply the payments to the purchase price. He wants $70,000 for the entire operation and real estate. The food and liquor inventory would be a separate purchase, about $7,000. The papers are being prepared. We'll go over and sign them when he gets them back from his lawyers, and then we have to apply for the liquor license."

Thought took over from astonishment as I absorbed the comparison between what Al was asking for the Fitzwilliam Inn and the $75,000 John King wanted for an inn less than half the size, with none of the accessories of pool or nearby skiing. Red continued, "He'd like us to get there as soon as possible because of Phyllis, so we decided the official takeover would be May 1. Quite a first anniversary gift to each other, isn't it?" I hugged him and congratulated his good fortune because, after all, it was his background and experience that Al was rewarding with his gift: I was only along for the ride

.Leaving Hancock

For this move, we hired a professional van and on the appointed day in late April John King positioned himself at the back door to watch the loading of the truck and be sure none of his possessions found their way on board. We had purposely kept our destination a secret from him, he knew only that we were purchasing our own place. Naturally he had to be concerned about the competition we would create because he knew Red's reputation and the following we had built up in Hancock during the months we had been there. In spite of his suspicious ways, he most certainly knew Red was a professional and commanded respect in his field.

Both Earle and the dishwasher, Jimmy Martin, were coming with us to Fitzwilliam. Earle had given his notice so John King must have suspected where he was going.

It was quite a little caravan as we drove out of Hancock. Red and I in the lead, with Jimmy in the back seat. Then came the moving van followed by Earle in his Saab. We headed down Route 137 to take the back way to Fitzwilliam through Dublin and Jaffrey. As we rounded a sharp curve, Red looked in his side-view mirror and exclaimed, "John King is back there! I can see the yellow Cadillac behind Earle!"

The Transition

The Bicknells were still occupying the manager's apartment, so our furniture was unloaded into the large room behind the kitchen and we took a guest room at the top of the back stairway. Red and Al had discussed the transition between innkeepers and, although Red knew Phyllis was extremely hostile to the sale, he felt it was important that the Bicknells be around for a week as we got acclimated.

In no time at all Earle and Bob Berry adjusted to one another. Earle had a natural instinct when it came to an authoritarian yet empathetic takeover which put Bob at ease. He consulted the younger man on favorite menu items, slowly introducing his own specialties. Jimmy Martin was given a small third floor room. Under Earle's guidance he began rearranging the dishes and cookware to make the food production a more efficient operation.

In mid-April I developed the following announcement which we mailed to friends, relatives and former customers in New Hampshire and Massachusetts.

Officially, we were to become the new innkeepers just one week ahead of the biggest single day of the year, Mother's Day. During the first week in May, the reservation book was overwhelmed with entries. Phyllis would cruise by the book and say "We never bothered to write all that down. Not necessary, when the food's gone, it's gone."

FITZWILLIAM INN		FITZWILLIAM N. H.
	An Inn Since 1796	

Hear ye and harken to our declaration,
For the news we impart is, in truth, a sensation!
We are proud to announce we've gone out on our own,
And are buying *this* Inn, which is very well known.
We will offer soft beds, a good grog and fine food,
In an atmosphere set for a jovial mood.
Plus added attractions — a pool and a Sauna,
And a patio set 'mid the flora and fauna.
If you're tired or hungry or have a great thirst
Please come to see us — we'll be there May 1st!

MARY LOU and ENOCH FULLER
Innkeepers

Red spent all his available time with Al trying to get a handle on statistical records of numbers served on holidays as well as popular entrees. Al had not kept this sort of information although he did have cartons of old dining room checks and bar slips. We *could* have sorted these out and recorded the information, but it was an overwhelming task. We had to begin our own history.

Phyllis

During the week I would be downstairs early to serve breakfast. The

Bicknells had a local high school girl on weekends, but weekdays were alarmingly informal. Phyllis appeared just as the dining room was to open in the morning and, plunging a hand down the front of her dress into the recesses of her bosom, she would locate the cash for the register. Once that was done she would again reach into her cleavage for the keys to lock the cash drawer. Rather than consider that perhaps I should have the keys, she promptly returned them to their hiding place.

As guests arrived for a meal she introduced me as the new owner, but en route to their table I could see her whispering conspiratorily, undoubtedly selling my shortcomings. When we were alone she was reluctant to share anything or permit me to take over the smallest task.

The second night of our residency, after an extremely long day, we had been in bed about an hour when pandemonium broke out below. The racket rose from the kitchen through the floor boards. We jumped up, grabbed robes and descended the back stairs. When we pushed open the door we were confronted by the sight of china platters, butter plates, "nappies", and soup cups - probably the entire service for one hundred and fifty - piled on the center of the kitchen work table. Pots, pans and mixing bowls were scattered across the floor. Phyllis, her feet shoved into muddy galoshes, hair standing out in disarray, was clumping from shelves to table and back again laden with what were now our china service and utensils. She was methodically undoing all Jimmy's work. Suddenly aware she was being watched, she looked at us and smiled, a twisted gesture with only half her face in control. Red went upstairs and called to Al. He came down, and with considerable severity, ordered her out of the kitchen.

Late at night before Mothers Day, we could hear furniture being moved downstairs and, although we figured Phyllis was at it again, we decided to  wait until morning to tackle the problem. When I got to the dining room for breakfast the tables were in their usual places but she had lined up all the chairs side-by-side. They stretched from the front door, through the dining room to the kitchen. It looked like preparation for musical chairs on a grand scale. I got busy putting things right before house guests showed up for breakfast. All the place settings had to be straightened and the chairs put back. As I moved from table to table towards the front of the room, I came upon Phyllis. She was stretched out under the table at the entrance to the dining room. Her head under one chair, her feet under the other. A half-empty highball glass was on the table where she had been sitting. I figured she had passed out and slithered off her chair onto the floor and was sleeping it off. Poor Al. He came down, got her up and led her away.

Phyllis was determined to keep up her disruptive tactics but she forgot we were now the "owners of record". Red finally urged Al to move out of the Inn. This man, who had been so generous to us, apologized profusely and said "You're only seeing a small part of what she's like." The next day they moved into a small apartment in a house they owned on the Upper Troy Road. However, they remained in Fitzwilliam for two more years while Al found and hired Dan Leary to run the ski area. Phyllis was never happy with the Inn whenever they came down for a meal. One winter evening when Red and I were taking a rare night off, she and Al arrived with guests. Even then, dressed in heels, hose and dinner dress, she re-arranged the stacks of firewood in the front rooms. Al finally sold all his holdings in Fitzwilliam and they moved to Sun City, Florida.

Al Bicknell's sign advertising new Pub and ski tow

Swimming Pool - Al Bicknell standing in water (center)

IV

BRAND ASS IRONS

The Routine

Once the Bicknells left the Inn, Red and I were able to settle in with less difficulty. We moved into the manager's apartment and began to feel like the innkeepers at last.

We established a work schedule that caused Red to say was "twenty-four hours a day, *eight* days a week"! It was important to keep labor costs down and there was no secret as to how this was accomplished: we did most of the work ourselves.

The PBX ruled my life in the early days. Overnight guests, amazed to discover that such an old inn had telephones in the rooms, quite naturally used them. Each time a receiver was picked up anywhere upstairs, the PBX would chatter and, regardless of where I was, I had to respond. Wake-up calls were a particular trial. I was too naive to tell guests "the switchboard doesn't open until eight in the morning", so I reported for duty when the first wake-up call was due; sometimes as early as six a.m. Often there would be just one call to make prompting me to say to Red, "Why can't we just hand them an alarm clock?"

Before the dining room opened for breakfast, I prepared the house guests' accounts for checkout: recording room, meal and Pub charges. I waited on table for breakfast from 8 to 9:30, made up the rooms and returned to the front desk by late morning to answer the mail and take reservations. The PBX would be blissfully quiet once the guests had checked out.

When Red came down later in the morning, he and Earle would talk over the day's meals, the food orders and upcoming special events. Then the menu information would be brought to me. We had created menu boards, replicas of horn books once used in Colonial school rooms. Instead of slates, we wrote the menu selections on colored paper and pinned them to the boards. Using an electric wood burning set, I had carved the Rebus onto the backs adding to their attraction. They were unique, a great gimmick and the guests loved them.

Red was the bartender during the week and I did all the hostessing seven days a week, all meals. In those days, in addition to plotting the reservations and seating the guests, hostessing also meant pouring water, dispensing butter pats, giving out menus and a three-part relish tray (that needed frequent replenishing) and a basket of crackers. This was time-consuming but Red felt it was important because it provided a great opportunity to chat with the guests.

Red's diabetes was always with us. It was amazing how fast insulin could get the upper hand in his system. His energy would be drained by the exercise he got just walking back and forth from Pub to kitchen for ice or liquor, carrying guests' bags upstairs or rushing for the PBX. It would be especially difficult for him if he was needed to clear tables and bus trays. Sometimes he would come to a complete stop in the middle of the dining room, seemingly rooted to the floor, moving his lips but making no sound. Oftentimes he would be holding a tray of dishes which would list alarmingly. I would rush to him, rescue the tray and lead him by the hand to the kitchen where Earle would sit him down and administer orange juice.

Red would be up most nights until at least midnight, if not on duty in the Pub then working in his office in our apartment. In addition to recording all receipts and expenses and paying the bills, he was creating an historical record of entrees, meals sold and numbers of advanced reservations for

---

RULES OF THE INN

HERE IN THE COUNTRY WE HAVE SOME RULES THAT WE HOPE YOU WON'T FIND TOO DIFFICULT TO FOLLOW

1. There are no locks on the room doors. However, the outside doors to the inn are locked at 11 p.m. If you are planning to be out after this hour, please pick up a key at the front desk - the innkeeper is bashful about answering the door in his pajamas.
2. If you need to be up early, we will be happy to lend you an alarm clock. Please stop at the desk.
3. In winter, there is a ski slope within walking distance right up Richmond Road. Please wait until you're outside the inn to put on your ski boots.
4. In summer we have a pool and Sauna out back. Please do not appear on the first floor in your bathing suit. Follow the second floor hall to the back stairs down to the Patio. Only plastic glasses are permitted around the pool.
5. Meal Hours:
   Breakfast Monday - Saturday 8-9:30 a.m.
   Sunday 8-10 a.m.
   Lunch Monday - Saturday Noon-2 p.m.
   Sunday Dinner Noon-2:30
   Dinner Monday - Saturday 6-9 p.m.
   Sunday Night Buffet 5-8 p.m.
   Reservations are recommended for Saturday night

IF THERE IS ANYTHING WE CAN DO TO MAKE YOUR STAY MORE ENJOYABLE, PLEASE LET US KNOW!

Mary Lou and Enoch Fuller
Innkeepers

holidays. This would be invaluable in years to come.

There were occasional nights after the Inn was locked and we had retired, that the front door bell would set off a buzzer over our bed that drove us instantly to our feet. We would pad through the Inn down to the front door. It was usually one of two situations: either a guest was inadvertently locked out or someone without a reservation needed a room. One night when we opened the door, a harried, mid-seventyish couple stood on the step. Seeing us in our nightclothes, they apologized profusely and explained, "We recently purchased a house in town, but we can't find the road." After hearing their general description of the locale, Red headed them in the right direction for Rockwood Pond, basking in the knowledge that he was indeed a full-service innkeeper!

After several months of this routine, we knew we were spreading ourselves too thin. It was one thing to keep the costs down and quite another to do the job right. As it was we were in constant motion, always excusing ourselves from a guest to dash off to something else. We concluded the PBX would have to go and with it the room phones. We had a pay telephone installed in the front office. We developed the "Rules of the Inn" which covered such things as wake-up calls and locked doors. We posted these notices in each guest room, purchased a supply of cheap alarm clocks and doubled the number of front door keys.

We took a hard look at which areas were robbing us of quality time as innkeepers. Two came to mind immediately. The first was housekeeping and the second was manning the front desk and answering the telephone during the lunch and dinner hours. In addition, we wanted to put a small gift shop in one side of the office.

The Mothers, Mimi and Abbie

The Mothers

We had two good jobs but could not afford to hire anyone to fill them. However, each of us had a mother. Would they be crazy enough to step into the breach and help us out? It turned out they would in return for their rooms and all they could eat. So began a ten-year association with two loving, but quite often incorrigible, seventy-year olds.

They came to the Inn with some common denominators: both had been raised on small New England farms, had not had very easy lives and now, either widowed or divorced and recently retired, they were living alone.

They shared a single purpose: to exude warmth and caring for our guests, the Inn itself and, most particularly, Red and me. They never failed to point to us with pride as we rushed about, trying to be "all things to all people".

Abbie, Red's mother, born and raised in Greenfield, was endowed with New Hampshire wit and wisdom. She had many friends and still some relatives in the area and knew all the local lore about the Monadnock region. When she arrived in Fitzwilliam as our housekeeper, she brought a sense of humor and vitality that soon made her an integral part of the Inn's personality. Her hearty laugh would often be heard ringing through the rooms upstairs as she encountered something that amused her or shared a joke with a guest or staff member.

Mimi, my mother, who was raised in Massachusetts, spent her married life in Haverford, Pennsylvania. More introverted than Abbie, she was at the same time charmingly cosmopolitan which reflected the twenty-plus years spent outside of rural New England. We could not have found a better match of individual to job than Mimi was for the gift shop and front desk.

Two Rooms, No Bath

At the hub of activity in the large front hall on the second floor were two adjacent single rooms with running water. These were assigned to the Mothers. Each room had the same peculiarity, other than its occupant. Because of their proximity to the joint caused by the connection of the two front buildings, the floors slanted down from the north side at an unsettling degree. When the ladies rose in the morning and headed out at a shuffle for the wash basin at the south side of the room, they would gather uncontrollable momentum, arriving at their sinks at a gallop.

Abbie took her bath around the corner from her room in the public facility that served all the guest rooms along the north side of the second floor rear. But Mimi's room connected to a double through a large bath which, along with her single, had at one time been rented as a suite. When the double room was vacant, Mimi enjoyed a private bath and would seize the opportunity to luxuriate in the lovely old tub. Before running her bath she always carefully checked the room reservation chart. In addition, she secured the lock on her side of the bathroom door. Red had warned her repeatedly about the chance she was taking but avoiding the trip to the public bath was worth the risk.

Her luck ran out one evening when the room was rented unexpectedly just as she had settled into the warm bath water. Escorted by Red, two women arrived in the double room next to where she was soaking. Mimi desperately tried to get out of the tub without splashing, but her knees would not cooperate. The only alternative was to sit very still and hope the guests would go down to dinner without needing their toilet. She lost out again when one of the women took hold of the doorknob and, when it failed to open, rattled and pulled as Mimi watched the hook and eye fastener jerk back and forth, praying it would hold. Finally, pronouncing the door "jammed" they went down to report it to the innkeeper. Breathing a sigh of relief, Mimi raised her puckered torso from the tub, cleaned up the bath and escaped to her room. She unfastened the hook to the connecting room and locked the door on her side.

Television

Abbie and Mimi both loved television and when evening came they would turn on the set in the front parlour and sit back to enjoy a show or two. If a house guest had beaten them to the TV they were often disgusted with the program. If this was the case, they would check the room register to see which of the two front bedrooms on the second floor was unoccupied. Since each of these had a television set, it was always a good second choice as a viewing locale. Neither Red nor I knew this was going on until there came a night when once again guests arrived without a reservation. Red's shock could only have been equalled by the Mothers' when he stepped into Room #3, guests in tow, to find his mother and mother-in-law each on a bed, shoes off, absorbed in _their_ choice of program. Red backed up, apologized for "his" error and dashed down to the office to check the chart for another vacant room. Meanwhile, the Mothers, thoroughly chagrined, gathered up their shoes and scurried up the hall to their rooms. There was nothing else for us to do but invest in two small TV's, one for each of them.

Once they had their own sets, they would retire to their rooms soon after things quieted down in the gift shop, get into bed and enjoy at least an hour of shows. Although they usually watched the same programs, they never considered getting together in one another's room, preferring instead to meet about 9:30 or 10 for refreshments. Clad in flowing bathrobes, they would simultaneously crack their doors and peek out to see if there was anyone in the hallway. As Abbie's hearing was poor, Mimi had the added responsibility of listening for approaching voices from downstairs. If the coast was clear, they set out for the back stairway, running the gauntlet of the guest room doors along that narrow hall where potential discovery lurked, planning to duck into the public bath at one end, or the large linen closet at the other if anyone appeared. Then, after stealing down the steep flight of steps, a treacherous undertaking even for those younger and more agile, they finally arrived in the kitchen. They employed the same "field" tactics on the return trip, only slightly hampered by their heaping dishes of ice cream.

Fulla Gifts

Mimi took great pleasure in the gift shop. She enjoyed ordering and pricing the inventory and tastefully arranging the stock on the shelves. I provided an old step ladder which she used to display jars of preserves and pickles. We mounted a small iron wagonwheel to a wall bracket where neckties and leather belts were hung. Most merchandise was handcrafted in New England, such as maple syrup, balsam pillows and note paper, but we also carried pewter jewelry, aprons, postcards and souvenir ashtrays with the Inn logo.

Mimi was very exacting when it came to balancing her sales slips with the gift shop cash register and was extremely proud that Red could pay his taxes from the annual profit made on the shop. She was in the big time.

The Pride of Mothers

Either Mother was always available to assist a guest with any problem or question they felt qualified to handle. Never too tired to heat a baby's bottle, fetch a glass of warm milk for an aging overnighter, fill in at a Canasta game and, in general, take the time to extend extra measures of hospitality which reflected our entire premise that we were entertaining in our own home.

We had a jigsaw puzzle going in the library year-round. It was a relaxing pastime for the guests and in the evening the Mothers would often stop to put in a piece or two. The guests saw this as an opportunity to get "close" to the Fullers and they were never disappointed as the Mothers took turns singing the praises of the innkeepers and providing tidbits of harmless gossip.

Of the two, it was Abbie who saw more corners of the Inn by the very nature of her position as head housekeeper. She took her son's reputation as a New Hampshire innkeeper of some note very seriously and was extremely protective of the Inn as well. She could be heard saying "I must go and report this at once" as she dashed downstairs to get to Red with the latest problem she had discovered. These usually ran the gamut of a shower curtain not kept inside the tub properly or too much toilet tissue being used.

She had to assemble all the dirty linen in one of the unused back rooms on the second floor. She called it the "hurricane room" because it tilted and slanted at such an angle from the building's joints that it gave the appearance of having come through a twisting gale. It was in this very hurricane room that she made her most famous discovery and was almost too speechless to report it.

A busload of teenagers arrived one winter Saturday for a ski outing to be followed by supper at the Inn. The skiing was rained out and the chaperones, not too creative with alternative pastimes, left the twenty young people to wander through town and pass the day unsupervised. We were constantly monitoring the kids and would ask each other, "Where on earth are the chaperones?" Much to Abbie's inexperienced and sheltered eyes, she found the missing pair in the hurricane room engaged in a sexually explicit activity on top of her bags of soiled bed linen. There was plenty of stormy tropic heat in the room that cold day and a lot for the Mothers to say about it in the library that evening.

Both Mimi and Abbie shared a self-imposed responsibility for reading outgoing postcards and all entries in the comments' section of the dining room guest book. We knew they were doing this and shuddered to think they might dare throw out a card. Red finally had to scold them when he discovered they had used a black magic marker to delete a humorous complaint in the guest book.

All Around the Town

The Mothers enjoyed Fitzwilliam and in the warm weather loved to sit out on the Inn's sweeping porches. They watched the guests come up the path to the steps, comparing notes on the size, shape and dress of each. These were the days of the miniskirt and there was lots to see.

They also took long walks, separately or together. Abbie's favorite was up to the ski area where, after the snows were gone, she would find wild flowers, four-leaf clovers and often a handful of change that had spilled out of the pocket of an unsuspecting skier who had "wiped out" on the slope.

Mimi liked to circle the grassy common in the center of Fitzwilliam. On one of her early walks she decided to take a look in some of the many antique shops across from the Inn. She entered the house on the corner which had lovely welcoming windows that reached from ceiling to floor on either side of the entrance. She knew this had once been a tea room and even now there were small tables, lovely dishes and a chair or two in these windows. Lost in her enjoyment of picking up dishes and examining the place of origin or maker, perusing book titles, scanning the pictures on the walls and even helping herself to a piece of candy thoughtfully laid out in an attractive sauce dish, she was startled by the sudden appearance of a young man who materialized from the back of the house. He looked equally as surprised as Mimi and, drying his hands on a towel asked, "Is there something I can do for you?" "Oh, no thank you," Mimi replied, "I'm just browsing." To her dismay he said, "This is not a shop; it's a private home!" She headed for the door, bowing and apologizing as she went and retreated to the safety of the Inn. It was several days before she could bring herself to share the story.

Probably the Mothers' most daring expedition was a walk up the Upper Troy Road and off onto a dirt track that led to the Pinnacle, the highest point in Fitzwilliam. Here they found an abandoned house, built and beautifully furnished by a retired couple who had lived in it only briefly. When the husband suddenly died, his widow, unable to bear the loneliness and seclusion during her grief, had fled leaving the closets stocked with linens, staples and dishes. Vandals had begun to prey on the lovely place, smashing in the windows and doors to gain access. The Mothers were drawn to it and entered the house through the gaping French windows. They were appalled at the destruction, and, thrifty Yankees that they were, set about to "save" what linens they could from future vandalism. They loaded their underclothes with dish towels, pillow slips, bureau scarves and other small items filling every nook and cranny of their brassieres and the tops of their stockings. Thoroughly padded, they waddled their way back down to the Inn. When they confessed, once again Red laid down the law. But the more he scolded, the more they gloated over their treasures; in the end they were right: the house with all its contents was destroyed by fire.

A Spoonerism to Remember

Abbie loved to talk to herself while she worked around the Inn and did it in a voice loud enough to satisfy her own faulty hearing. One day I heard her unmistakable monologue coming from one of the front rooms on the second floor. There were fireplaces in each of these and Abbie took pride in keeping the brass andirons shining. As I approached, it was easy to tell she was busy at her polishing: "Such a lovely pair of brand ass irons," she said. Her unwitting spoonerism struck me funny and I retraced my steps without interrupting her. It was my turn to go and report to Red.

V
IF THE GRATE BE FULL

A 175 Year Old Friend

Red and I were proud of the Inn and its far-reaching reputation for good food and warm hospitality. We had inherited a business that had been nurtured down through the years, passing from one devoted innkeeper to another.

In earlier days the Boston train stopped at the Depot south of the village. Here the city folk would be met by horse-drawn coaches and driven up the hill to the Inn. The season had always been June to October and it was not until 1959 that business had been done year-round.

Now, population explosions and easy credit plans had crowded the highways with automobiles and, by the mid-1960's, the travel and dining out boom was beginning. It did not take long for Red and me to almost double the gross dollars the Bicknells had done; they did not need the money and we did: the Inn was our livelihood as well as our home.

As business increased, so did the traffic through the building. Every floorboard, plumbing fixture and electrical connection felt a terrific strain, but because we were so involved with the day-to-day operation, we failed to understand what our "old friend" was suffering. Although Al had done much to enhance the Inn with the modern accessories of patio, pool, sauna and Pub, he told us frankly that he had never looked beneath the surface for support systems that might need replacing or improvement. It would not be long before the "old girl" started to complain.

Paper and Paint

One thing *was* very obvious: the outside of the building was extremely shabby. The paint was chipped, peeling and non-existent in some places. The clapboards were in danger of rotting and needed immediate attention. It would be an enormous job even for a professional and we shuddered at the potential cost. We had not considered local painters because we were too new in town to have made that discovery. Luckily, the painters found us and a friendship and working relationship between Red, Warren Spicer and Eric Wentworth began. Neither Warren nor Eric had ever tackled a painting job of this magnitude but Eric, a retired Bosun's Mate, knew about painting the sides of naval vessels and Warren understood scaffolding and construction. We chose a pale Colonial yellow with white trim and black shutters. When the job was done the entire town felt rejuvenated and we were pleased with the favorable comments that came our way.

The hallways also needed brightening and refurbishing. We selected wallpaper with a Williamsburg print in Colonial red against a neutral background and decided to paint the wainscotting neutral, with the chair rail a matching red. All thoughts of being able to afford the luxury of hiring outside help for this job had to be discarded: it was simply too costly. The multi-talented Bob Berry, who had never done any wallpapering, volunteered to head up the project and Abbie immediately signed on as his assistant. Red and I would do the painting. One quiet December evening signalled the start of stripping the old paper from the walls in the third floor hall. Recalling the upside down paper in the dining room, we decided this

far corner would make early mistakes more difficult to detect. Red purchased a top of the line cutting board for Bob; the best paste and brushes. I had the paint mixed and delivered, gallon after gallon. We were underway.

Abbie and Bob settled into a routine of sorts with their papering. First, they both carefully measured the wall which was a devilish task in itself. The settling of the building over time caused serious irregularities, and the measurements varied so widely that loud arguments and much name calling broke out each time they prepared to cut the wallpaper. By the same token, once a strip was successfully pasted and hung, a celebration followed which involved Bob waving his paste brush in triumph and whacking Abbie several times with it for good measure. She, in turn, would go into gales of laughter, then wash off the cutting board and prepare to argue the measurement and placement of the next piece. Her work dress, already a patched relic, eventually became a "cotton mâché" monument to her task. Molded with paste from Bob's triumphant brush, it could stand *alone* in her closet as the final days of the enormous undertaking drew to a close.

The painting, however, hit an early snag. Red was blessed with two left hands when it came to any form of manual dexterity. He had told me this before, but faced with painting the Inn's hallway wainscotting and doors by myself, I tossed aside good judgment and asked him to take part. All went smoothly as we painted our way along the third floor hall. The next area was the stairway that led down to the second level. We carefully spread out a drop cloth to protect the red stair carpet and settled in to work on the balusters. Red was behind me on a higher step, dressed as always in shirt and tie, but wearing a Sherwin Williams paint cap "to set the mood", he said. I had poured a small amount of paint from the gallon container into a coffee can which was easier for me to manage; Red had scoffed at that idea and was dipping directly into the mother load. We were working in silent concentration when suddenly I heard a muffled "Uh, oh" and at the same time, out of the corner of my eye saw a trickle of paint heading my way from above. The latex, like lava, thickened and menaced as it traversed the drop cloth. I jumped up and saw the gallon can upside down and Red frantically gathering up his corners of the cloth trying to halt the flow as it crept downward. His hat was

askew; his glasses had slipped to the end of his nose. "Help me!" he croaked. I grabbed my corners of the drop cloth and somehow we corralled the brute which gurgled and gulped. Issuing orders to each other all the way, we managed to wrestle the awkward load to the closest bathtub. Red was covered to his elbows with paint and his loafers and slacks were splattered. He was beginning to perspire and I knew he was in danger of an insulin reaction so I suggested he go clean up while I dealt with the mess. I never urged him to help again.

By the time Bob, Abbie and I had worked our way to the first floor we were a confident, coordinated crew. The end result of the entire project was a remarkable improvement and provided hours of hilarious recollection whenever we recounted our amazing task.

Electricity

As much as we hated to admit there was a problem, the electrical power coming into the building was not adequate for the business we were doing. To add to the increased usage, we had purchased a new refrigerator for Earle and a routine inspection by the fire marshall resulted in the installation of a more powerful exhaust system for the Fryolater. We were also told we needed a new fan to maintain the cold temperature in the walk-in box. By the very nature of its name, this was a huge refrigerator used to hang sides of beef as well as the storage of other foods.

In addition to keeping on top of food production, Earle had to keep his mind on which appliances he should unplug whenever he needed to run the fans. If he forgot, the fuses would blow reducing the entire building to darkness. It always seemed to happen in the evening at the height of the dinner hour.

House guests would appear saying, "I hate to bother you when you're busy, but the lights are out in my room"; or, "I can't use my shaver"; or worse, "My wife's hair is wet, full of rollers and her dryer won't turn on."

Both Red and I had become adept at changing fuses; but one night when the front hall was unexpectedly plunged into darkness, two waitresses collided as they served a cocktail party in the parlour. They were not hurt but two tray-loads of expensive drinks were wasted. The electrician was finally called in.

We dreaded the outcome of his estimate but were not in the least prepared when he told us there were only 100 amps coming into the entire compound of buildings and the kitchen *alone* was using 175. Subsequently, a total re-wiring of the Inn was accomplished. Because it was not a visible improvement, and had taken a considerable toll on our resources, Red enjoyed telling our house guests, "Enjoy the new electricity; the transition from oil lamps was completed just before you arrived."

Water

The Inn had its own artesian well located just outside the Pub windows on the north side of the building. It produced delicious clear cold water. The supply was more than adequate for all our needs.

When the pool was built, a fault in the formula governing the mixture of sand and cement resulted in a porous condition. This allowed water to leak out and back in, depending on the level of the water table. We kept the hose attached to the spigot in the bathhouse so water could be constantly added. We sought advice from pool experts for miles around on how to cure the leaking. We applied their sealers and installed their liners but nothing helped and eventually we stopped spending money on consultations and ineffective treatments. We drained the pool as best we could each October but, because the deep end was below the frost line, the water continued to leak in during the winter. When this froze, the resulting expansion threatened to cause serious cracking. To avert that problem railroad ties were put in the pool. Red tried to explain the physics principle saying, "The wooden ties absorb the expansion," but it was difficult for me to grasp.

In the spring, after the ground thawed, we had a half-filled pool of dirty water. Then began the tortuous task of draining, cleaning and painting for the summer season. One person would clean and paint while just ahead, two more wielding buckets, bailed out the water.

The water temperature never rose above 65 degrees: the heat of the sun could not get ahead of the cold water that kept arriving from the well. It was a shock to some guests who always wanted to know why we didn't heat it; but others, who enjoyed the sauna, appreciated being able to go from the dry heat to the extremely cold water.

The same underground springs that plagued the pool also caused problems in the cellar under the original part of the Inn. This building sat on a dirt floor covered with layers of gravel. Whenever we had a hard rain, the underground waters would reach flood level and rush through the cellar rising to heights that threatened to snuff out the boiler. David Payea, friend, neighbor and creative troubleshooter, traced the water's entrance and dug a trench in the gravel from there to a point where the water was forced to exit. This worked well except in bitter cold when the exiting water froze solid and formed a large mound of ice on the edge of the road just off the front of the Inn. Not to be outdone, Dave dug other trenches in subsequent winters until we had a network of rivulets below, each with its own exit. This reduced the size of the original ice mound; now we were ringed with a series of small ones. At least the boiler survived.

More Water

The question of which innkeeper had added the small guest rooms on the north side of the back hall was never resolved. The metal showers in the two public bathrooms that served these rooms were a constant problem. An inadvertent bump of the sides while showering set off a gong-like reverberation heard throughout the second floor. But the major complaint was with the shallow lip that was supposed to contain the water. It made no difference how many warning notices Abbie posted *"to keep the curtain inside"*, because that was only a small part of the problem. It was the amount and power of water preferred by the individual user. Short of having Abbie accompany each guest to the bath and personally adjust the water, there was no way to control it.

These two bathrooms were located over the dining room. If a "high water pressure" person was showering, the water would quickly overflow and run to the lowest part of the slanting room, seep through the floor boards and, if we were lucky, stay there. Invariably, if the dining room was busy, the water kept coming until it had dripped through to the dining room below. It usually landed on the floor between tables and that was bad enough; but when it sought out the center of a table, and once to our horror a plateful of smoked pork chops, Red and I would be devastated.

The guests jumped up, waitresses raced for buckets and cloths. Meanwhile the innocent perpetrator showered on, blissfully ignorant of the chaos below. Abbie, ever alert to real or imagined disasters, took care of that in a hurry. Arriving at the bathroom she would bang on the door and order the occupant to "shut off the water at once" and then insist on getting in to mop up the mess.

Eventually the embarrassed guest would slink down to the dining room only to be confronted by the sight of our kitchen pails still collecting the shower water from "on high."

We could not keep people from using these facilities so we endured, promising ourselves that we would install proper showers one day when other, more urgent areas were attended to.

Plumbing

Next to the re-wiring, we spent more money on plumbing repairs than anything else. It was a never-ending battle and we were always on the losing side.

The Inn had two septic systems, each serving different buildings in the complex. The larger of the two was across the street where the old inn once stood. Waste from all but the original Inn traveled under both the north lawn and the Lower Troy Road to get to its final destination; a distance of approximately seventy-five yards. The smaller and original system accommodated the bulk of the guest rooms and public toilets in the main building. This was situated just outside the dining room windows on the south side. Neither of these systems was designed for the increased heavy use they were getting, having been installed to handle a summer operation only.

We had already experienced some minor plumbing problems in the kitchen but nothing compared with the obstruction that occurred somewhere in the seventy-five yard span between kitchen and septic system. Roto-rooter stood by while the plumber sought out the problem. What he found was unbelievable. There were two drainage pipes making the trip to the system and these were deep underground well below the frost line. So deep, that the persons installing the swimming pool and the flagstone patio never knew they positioned these two additions directly over the pipes.

In order to make the repairs, the pipe had to be re-routed: the section with the obstruction was under the shallow end of the pool and severing the pipe was the only solution. Therefore, a trench had to be excavated around the entire circumference of bathhouse and swimming pool and back to the point where the pipe could be re-joined on the north side.

A few years later, plumbing under the patio suffered a similar clog and to reach it we had to choose between a jack hammer or an electric drill with a diamond cutter. Left with the choice of destroying one end of the patio or neatly removing a few flagstones, we spent the several hundred dollars an hour to rent the diamond cutter.

A Horse in the Ladies' Room

The septic system outside the dining room was in full view of the four popular deuce tables. Those of us who knew it was there cringed when it quietly bubbled to the surface, never knowing what to expect. It was always worse on rainy days when the water from above saturated the ground thwarting the work of the small leach field.

The Inn was a popular luncheon spot for fall foliage bus tours. These were usually senior citizen clubs from around Boston and, because Fitzwilliam was only two hours from the city, lunch at the Inn was ordinarily the first stop. Golden-aged internal plumbing, bounced along on a sixty mile bus ride, could soon reach "flood level". Such was the case one particular day.

Predominantly a female group, the first off the bus made a beeline for the ladies' room followed closely by her fellow female passengers until there was a close-rank line from our two-stall facility out the door of the Inn and down the granite steps. We never understood whether or not fear of losing one's place in line was the motivation, but no doors, except those to the stalls were ever closed; on the other hand, no time was lost having to open any. This concentrated use severely challenged the ancient plumbing to such an extent the toilets refused to cooperate at all.

When Abbie went into the facility to tidy up, she came rushing out repeating her familiar line, "I must go and report this at once". Bob Berry returned with her and in a few minutes streaked by the Pub where Red and I were getting drinks for the bus group. He was waving his arms over his head in disbelief saying, "There's been a horse in the ladies' room!" It *was* a dreadful sight but Bob, armed with plunger, bucket and mop, attacked the problem with his usual vigor. Long afterwards, Red would tell how he knew the exact minute and second that Bob gained the upper hand: a three-foot geyser sprang from the septic system, blowing debris out onto the lawn. He described how he held his breath and shut his eyes, afraid to look. Then he hurried to put "reserved" signs on the deuce tables to keep them unoccupied until Bob could get outside with a wheelbarrow of sand to spread on the lawn.

If the Grate Be Full

August could be damp and rainy and one Saturday during our first year in Fitzwilliam the temperature dipped to the 60's. The Mothers were working on a jigsaw puzzle in the library and, although the Olde Rebus over the fireplace called for coal if the "grate be empty", there was no fire to keep them warm. We had a college boy working for us that summer as sort of a general all-around helper. He saw them huddled over the card table and asked if they would like a fire. The Mothers were delighted, unaware that the chimneys had not been cleaned in several years. Randy piled on the logs until he had a sizable blaze and the thick soot that had collected in the chimney caught fire almost immediately. A guest coming in from outside, reported flames shooting from the top of the chimney. When Red went into the library he could hear the roar of the fire up inside and shouted to me to call mutual aid. The fire department responded quickly and, using a steam blower, had everything extinguished promptly. In the follow-up investigation, holes were discovered in a section of the chimney that ascended up through the closet in Room #27, the front room on the third floor. The fire easily could have broken through these chinks and from there to the roof: the entire Inn could have been lost.

Continued Care for An Old Friend

The most costly physical plant improvements Red and I put into the

Fitzwilliam Inn were the result of near disasters and none was evident to the naked eye. But because of our love for the old place and what it represented to us, we never considered ignoring any of its needs: it was all part of keeping an inn.

Library with Olde English Rebus

46

VI
DON'T WORRY ABOUT A THING

Changing Hands

It is not unusual for staff members to find the transition difficult when a business passes from one owner to another. A few of the Bicknell's employees fell into this category, all for the same reason: they could not deal with Red's professional methods and resented the constraints he placed on them. He insisted on punctuality and dependability, had a sensory perception about the validity of the excuses for tardiness or absence and felt if they wanted to work for us, they *had* to work. Al Bicknell made no secret that, for him, the Inn was a hobby and a tax write-off and he paid no attention to costs. This attitude was reflected throughout the Inn when we arrived and Red had to turn it around. Waitresses who felt their tips would suffer if they could no longer heap ice cream on a guest's pie, instead of the single scoop we allowed, turned in their aprons.

Earle was also a complete professional. He was fussy about how waitresses presented their orders to him. Especially strict about handwriting, he was aware that illegibility caused mistakes in what *he* prepared and *they* served, resulting in money lost. Red paid him a monthly bonus to keep the food cost on an even keel and Earle took this incentive very seriously. He watched over the waitresses, second cook and baker while they worked, correcting any serving size that seemed too large or small. At the same time, he carefully weighed and measured the entrees he personally prepared until he could accurately "eyeball" a portion size. If a new menu item was created, he and Red discussed the cost of ingredients for a generous serving in order to arrive at a fair retail price. Earle was invaluable in both knowledge and ability, never abusing his position or threatening to "pack up his knives" and leave to force us into a pay increase. He was a good man, even-tempered and, as a chef, had the respect of the staff and the Fullers.

Waitresses

It was important that our food and beverages be presented with the care and attention necessary to create the illusion that we were entertaining in our own home. Therefore, we looked upon the waitresses as an extension of ourselves and regarded their service as an intimate contact with the guests.

Although Sally Wear was a carryover from Al and Phyllis, through the years she became the backbone of our serving staff. Sally approached working for us as if she were in business for herself. She took an interest in the parties she served without "hovering" and provided the quality of gracious service that anticipated the customers' needs. She was fascinating to watch and I learned much about service efficiency from her. Red and I appreciated her on-the-job performance and her loyalty to us and the Inn.

In summer we took on several high school girls to augment our waitress staff. New hires were usually assigned to "shadow" Sally for a few meals to learn the kitchen routine and, hopefully, pick up some of her techniques. Once in a while this resulted in over-eager service as the young girls struggled to please. Red loved to repeat the story told by one of our guests who ordered an extra dry Martini and the neophyte responded "I'll have the bartender use dry ice."

All of the waitresses wore white uniform dresses. To this was added a checkered apron. They came in all colors, were smocked with white stitching across the waistband and were known as "Fitzwilliam aprons" because they were made locally. The current miniskirt fad caused problems for Red when he spotted an exposed girdle on a "short skirted" waitress. Knowing this did nothing to enhance the Inn's early American ambiance, he issued a "henceforth mid-knee length uniform decree."

New waitresses were all required to serve a lunch or dinner to Red and me before they were assigned "live" customers. This was a tough test because Red was particular and would say, "Anyone can *land* a plate of food and a cup of coffee; but a trained server *presents* a meal."

Don't Worry About A Thing

If there was a star of our show, other than Red and the Mothers, it was Bob Berry. Orphaned as a child, he was raised in Fitzwilliam by his aunt and uncle, Jenny and Phil, with whom he still lived. This couple were town natives and Phil, like many of his peers, took the opposing view on every improvement issue raised at the annual town meeting. This was largely because most proposals were made by what he referred to as "fur collar types": newcomers. Phil saw no reason to change a town that had been good enough for him for over seventy years. Extending his arms overhead in his classic gesture, flapping his hands for emphasis, Bob would act out his uncle's reactions to zoning, historic districts, recreation commissions and planning boards. We would be fascinated, tears of laughter running down our faces, all the while secretly doubting the truth of the stories; but only until we attended a town meeting ourselves and saw Uncle Phil shake his fist at the moderator and shout, "If a junk dealer set up next to me it's *his* business, not mine and shouldn't be yours either."

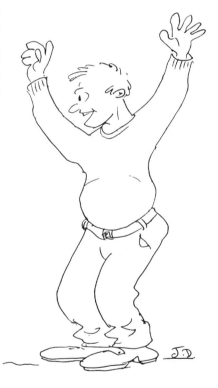

Bob was in his mid-twenties when we purchased the Inn. Given to a pot belly even then, his pants rode at the danger level on his hips, seemingly kept from slipping further by the excess material that trapped them around his ankles. He had a round, happy face and a generally carefree attitude. Red encouraged him to learn everything he could about the business. As a result, Bob was not only a talented second cook, taking over completely on Earle's day off, but was an excellent bartender and front-desk clerk. Guests liked him immediately. He had the ability to come up with a dry New Hampshire comment about most situations, usually turning difficulties into something humorous. He had wonderful stories to tell about people in town and, if true, Peyton Place had nothing on Fitzwilliam.

Bob's prescription for every crisis, regardless of its magnitude, was "Don't worry about a thing" and he spread this advice liberally.

A Friend is Lost

Jimmy Martin, the black dishwasher, had been an excellent part of our kitchen crew. However, his nightly chanting and candle burning had continued since Hancock days. He maintained an aloof but friendly relationship with everyone. When Lyndon Johnson signed the Civil Rights Amendment suddenly, before the president's ink was dry, Jimmy changed.

It happened one afternoon when he casually strolled out of the kitchen, through the dining room and into the Pub. I was sitting at a table in the Pub working on plans for an upcoming party. Jimmy appeared in the doorway. "All right do I sit with you and we have a drink?" I was lost for words. We knew about the Civil Rights Amendment, but Jimmy had made his move so quickly I had no idea how to respond. Was he asking as a friend? Was he daring me to refuse? He must have read the dismay in my face because he said, "Why won't you drink with me? Law say I have a right to be in here." I replied, "But the law doesn't say I have to drink with you. You know Red doesn't like any of the staff drinking in here. Is this about Civil Rights?" Jimmy shuffled around a bit then looked me in the eye and put more words together than I had ever heard him say at one time. "You knows it is. I been waitin' and prayin' for this day like all the Brothers and Sisters. Now We free - to go anywhere, sit anywhere: We entitled. I been burnin' my candles regular and it paid off. But I can't stay here no more: goin' back to Boston." He took off his apron and handed it to me. I stared at the doorway for many minutes after he left. "How sad," I thought, "he expected instant change." Jimmy left a large void in our midst and it was many days before we recovered from the strong sense of loss.

Frank

Bob and I managed to keep up with the dishwashing while we waited for someone to answer Red's help-wanted advertisement. It was not long before a teenager was hired; his name was Frank. Perhaps I was guilty of comparing him to Jimmy, but he had a sullen attitude which I disliked. Earle had trouble with Frank immediately over his failure to do a thorough job of washing the pots. The waitresses complained that the silverware was coming back spotted and still soiled. Red spoke to Frank about the importance of clean dishes and utensils and told him, "Show some improvement

or I'll have to let you go." Nothing changed. The next day he returned to the kitchen and told Frank to leave. As Red exited by way of the swinging door, Frank shouted, "Son of a bitch! You can shove your job!" Red made a quick turn, revolving back into the kitchen; but Frank was waiting for him, dishwashing hose in hand. Squeezing the nozzle trigger, he caught

Red full in the face with a tremendous spray of water, knocking off his eyeglasses and soaking his shirt and tie. Then, suddenly afraid of the consequences, Frank dashed across the kitchen and bolted out the door. The last we saw of him he was running up the road away from the Inn.

Red concluded the arrangement we had with Jimmy was as close to ideal as we could get. Economically, it was definitely in our favor to have the dishwasher live in and let room and board form a major portion of the salary. Supplemented by a small hourly rate, this worked out to be an ideal arrangement for the right man. It had to be a single person, older, semi-retired even; but needing housing. Red spoke to Mrs. Donovan, at the New Hampshire Unemployment Office in Keene and described the job and live-in requirement with its advantages. Neither Red nor Mrs. Donovan realized how many conversations they were going to have about dishwashers for the Fitzwilliam Inn.

Rodney Joseph Fisher

"He likes to be called Rodney Joseph," I was told when I arrived at the state office to pick up our new dishwasher. He had been described as older, late 50's, and eager to be independent. "He's in good health as far as I know; has a touch of asthma, but nothing serious enough to restrict the requirements of dishwashing," Mrs. Donovan had said.

Rodney's body canted rearward when he walked, a posture obviously designed to counterbalance an oversized paunch protruding through the straps of his red suspenders. I showed him the room assigned to him on the third floor and waited while he put away his belongings. On the return trip downstairs, I pointed out the public bathroom in the back hall of the second floor and explained that it was designated for employee use during the workday because of its convenience to the kitchen.

The next day near the end of lunch, Red and I sat down to eat. Our table, the first in the row of deuces, was strategically located: I sat facing the dining room in order to watch over the service while Red, on the opposite side, could keep an eye on the Pub and front entrance hall. That is how I happened to see Rodney come through the swinging door from the kitchen, headed in our direction. He was wearing his full-length kitchen apron, the entire paunch area was covered with unappetizing stains left by the dishes and pots he had washed during the day. I was speechless as he disappeared into the men's room next to the office. I should have warned Red, but his experience with Frank was still fresh in my mind: I knew how strenuously he could react.

It was not until Rodney began his return trip that Red got the picture of the soiled, wet apron. He leaped from his chair and hissed, "Rodney Joseph, don't ever come through the dining room again wearing an apron. Why aren't you going upstairs to the toilet?" Rodney replied, "I just can't keep climbing those steep stairs, Mr. Fuller. I get short of breath." "Well, go back to the kitchen," Red told him, "but that apron is a disgrace. Hold it up."

That night at dinner, after an extremely busy evening, Red and I once again settled at our table. The dining room was still fairly busy. We were eating our salads when I saw the kitchen door swing open and Rodney's shape once again loomed into view. "No apron," I thought, "that's good." Then, "Oh! My, God!" I watched in horror as, one by one, the guests caught sight of him, nudged each other and chuckled. Rodney, following orders, had left his apron in the kitchen but, not being able to see over his belly, had missed his trousers; the red suspenders were fastened to his brightly flowered boxer shorts causing the front of his trousers to gape and sag. I could hear him wheezing as he approached. I glanced at Red to see if he noticed the guests' tittering but when he did not react I said quietly, "Rodney needs help." Red jumped from his chair, took in the incredible sight, and in two strides had a grip on Rodney's arm, reversing his direction and escorting him back through the dining room and into the kitchen. The guests howled with laughter, thoroughly enjoying the impromptu entertainment.

When Red returned to the table he told me that Rodney Joseph was leaving. "He not only has asthma which makes the stairs difficult, but he has a urinary problem too. I'll call Mrs. Donovan in the morning."

Over the phone the next day, Red described Rodney's problems and said we were in the market for a replacement. Mrs. Donovan mentioned receiving an application that morning from a much younger man. "In his thirties," she said. "He recently had some personal problems, but otherwise is fine and looking for a place exactly like yours".

Ralph Jenkins

"His name is Ralph Jenkins," I was told when I arrived at the unemployment office to drop off Rodney and collect our new recruit. Ralph was a small man, thin, with deep, dark shadows under his eyes. He had little to say on the ride from Keene.

This time Red took over the orientation duties, showing Ralph his room and bath on the third floor and the staff toilet on the second. He also took considerable time to explain the work routine and even went a step further to describe the bus service that connected Keene, Fitzwilliam and Boston as something to consider on days off. Red told me later that there was a look of despair in Ralph's eyes, "almost as if he had reached the end; of what, I can't say."

The next morning brought Red's ESP into focus. When Ralph failed to put in an appearance by 9 a.m., Abbie decided to go wake him. Arriving at his room, she knocked and called, but received no reply. Opening the door a crack, she peered in and was met by a grisly sight. Ralph sat on the foot of the bed. He was leaning forward, both arms resting over the open top drawer of a low bureau. Blood poured into the drawer from the slashes he had made on the inside of both elbows. Abbie made a dash for the stairs. "Mary Lou! Mary Lou! Get an ambulance," she screamed, "Ralph's bleeding desperately."

I sprang for the front office telephone and dialed mutual aid and reported that our dishwasher was bleeding and needed immediate medical assistance. Afraid of what I would find, my heart tearing at my chest, I raced upstairs. Abbie was coming out of Ralph's room heading for the bath next door, a bundle of blood-soaked towels held at arm's length. Tears of helplessness and despair ran down her face. "He's cut his elbows," she said. "I've got his arms wrapped in towels but we'll need more. These are soaked." I grabbed towels from other rooms and hurried back with them. Abbie had managed to move Ralph to the floor where he lay pale and quiet; eyes closed. It seemed only minutes before Red rushed in followed by the Fitzwilliam Rescue Squad volunteers; the ambulance attendants were close behind. It was a super-human task for the men to both lift and tilt the stretcher to make their way down the steep, narrow stairs. "He's still alive," Red told us. "A miracle. He must have lost pints of blood. If you'd been a minute later, Abbie, he *would* have bled to death. Poor fellow, I was right: he had come to the end. Let's pack up his things and I'll drive up to the hospital then go tell Mrs. Donovan. What a record; two dishwashers in three days." He admonished his mother about not trying to clean the room. "We'll get Servicemaster," he told her. He had barely left before she began taking up the scatter rugs and whispering to herself that the blood would be "set" if she didn't start on it right away. Amazing as it seemed, Ralph survived his suicide attempt and was placed under psychiatric care.

We had a three-week hiatus with no full-time dishwasher so we hired high school boys for the dinner meals. Because Bob and I did breakfast and lunch dishes, in conjunction with all our other work, we barely finished cleaning up after one meal before the dining room opened again for the next.

Joe Morton

Red held fast in his resolve to find a live-in dishwasher; he knew *someone* out there would be a perfect match. Mrs. Donovan described Joe Morton as 60-ish, widowed and anxious to move out of his daughter's home in Keene. She had a family and career, and she was an EMT for mutual aid. Joe explained shortly after he arrived, "She's fussed over me like one of her kids since my wife died, insisting I move in with her so she could feed me and do my laundry. I retired early from Nembalite in Brattleboro. My wife and I were going to have a wonderful time, but sadly it was too late for her."

Joe was tall, healthy looking and good-humored. He quickly became a part of the Inn family. Earle was pleased with him and, on nights when we had no second cook, Joe would step over and garnish plates or perform other small tasks. It was unusual for the chef and dishwasher to be as compatible as Earle and Joe came to be.

About a year later, I was in the front office and heard Earle's unmistakable gait approaching from the dining room. Before coming into sight he began speaking in a loud, carefully enunciated voice, "You better call mutual aid, I think Joe's gone. He went over backwards behind the dish machine. No warning. No sound. I felt for a pulse: nothing."

I quickly put in the call and then hurried to the kitchen to assess matters. When he fell, Joe had somehow managed to wedge himself under the dish machine in such a way that both his head and feet were hidden from view. I got on my knees, reached under him and pulled his wallet from the back pocket to look for his daughter's telephone number. Just then the Fitzwilliam Rescue Squad and Mutual Aid crew came through the swinging door from the dining room. Right away one of them said, "That's Karen's dad. Boy, I'm glad she wasn't on call today."

The emergency vehicles were at the side entrance of the Inn, the attendants having assumed they were to carry someone from the dining room or a room upstairs. Thus it was that Red, driving up from Jaffrey saw the flashing red lights and commotion at the front of the Inn. He thought immediately of the Mothers. Leaving his car parked behind the ambulance he ran up the granite steps, coattails flying. Out of breath and on the brink of an insulin reaction, he was met inside by the Mothers, both hale and hearty but bearing the sorrowful tidings of Joe Morton. Abbie took Red into the Pub, sat him down and poured out a glass of orange juice.

There was a feeling of emptiness in our midst for quite some time akin to when Jimmy left. Joe had been like family and had become a concerned and unselfish co-worker. He was intensely missed.

Summer was at hand and we had no trouble attracting teenage boys from town to do dishes. However, Red was right as usual - they had no commitment to doing a good job and were primarily interested in getting through the noon hour so they could go for a swim. The waitresses only succeeded in bringing out the worst in adolescent rudeness as they tossed back unclean dishes and silverware. We were all glad to see Labor Day and the opening of school even though it meant a return to making do without a regular dishwasher.

Wendell Hadley

We were facing October and foliage season, our busiest time of the year. It was then our baker, Bessie Parker, told Earle all about Wendell Hadley. He relayed Bessie's story to Red.

Wendell came to the Parkers as a foster child and, as an adult, had continued to make his home with them, doing odd jobs and helping around the house. He had severely deformed feet and Bessie prevailed on the state to obtain the necessary orthopedic surgery which left him with just a heel on the left foot. The other leg ended in a stump at the ankle. A wooden, foot-shaped plug was fashioned for his "good left leg" which, when placed in his shoe, provided support and balance for the other on which he wore a prosthesis.

According to Bessie, Wendell got around quite well. "He's not had much schooling; but he's done dishwashing jobs and I think he could do this one. He'd love to live here, has no bad habits and is real clean. He's almost 40 and never had a chance in life. He's a bit of a character, but I'm here most everyday and that would get him started off right."

Long before quotas and affirmative action, Red never hesitated to hire the handicapped. He found those less able-bodied like himself tended to put more into their work. He agreed to talk to Wendell.

We both took to the little man with the elfin face, big ears and spike hair. Wendell readily demonstrated that he could travel the stairs by going one at a time. He also showed us he could carry a loaded tray from the dish machine across to the kitchen shelves and into the dining room. Earle felt we should give him a chance.

He was a combination of leprechaun and Pinocchio: above the waist, lively and excited about everything, as if entering the world for the first time; puppet-like from the hips down, he teetered dangerously, always on the brink of tipping over. He loved his work and did it well. Spotlessly clean about

Wendall with the Mothers and Mary Lou

himself, the trait was reflected in everything he touched. The waitresses were ecstatic. Red boasted that the kitchen floor, an unpainted wooden nightmare to keep clean, had turned into a miracle of spotlessness under Wendell's ministrations.

On his day off, Bessie would take him home overnight. He would return the next morning, his bag of laundry slung over his back. Wendell's delight over his freedom knew no bounds. If he wanted to sit up late on the porch and smoke, he did. If he found an especially garish sport shirt on a shopping trip, he bought it. He ate well. He socialized with anyone who would listen. Then one day Bessie announced she was moving to Connecticut to live with her sister. Wendell was forced to make a choice between going with his foster mother or staying at the Inn. He opted for independence.

Completely naive about the amount of guidance and control Wendell required, Red and I agreed to keep him on, provide a home and tend to his personal needs, such as laundry, doctor visits and so forth. We would have agreed to almost anything to avoid losing him. And so, he was ours for better or worse.

Because he did his work in such stellar fashion, it was hard to realize that Wendell had difficulty making sound decisions. Like Pinocchio, he wanted to be a real man and reached out to the wrong people to help him achieve this goal. On his first day off after Bessie left, he announced he was taking the bus to Winchendon to do his laundry. This sounded like a good idea, so we let him go not realizing he had his pay check with him. When the dining room closed that evening, Earle mentioned that Wendell had not returned and offered to drive to Winchendon to check around. He returned an hour later with Wendell in the car. He just happened to see him lying on the side of the road drunk; all his money was gone and so was his laundry. Sober he could barely control his wobbling legs, inebriated it was a lost cause; he was forced to crawl up the three flights of stairs to his room on his hands and knees.

The next day I drove down to the Curve In, a seedy bar perched on a bend in the road on Route 12 south of Fitzwilliam, just over the line into Massachusetts. The laundry bag was still there. The bartender said Wendell had come in with a man who had given him a lift from the laundromat and had told Wendell he would be "one of the guys" if he bought everyone a drink. So he had willingly treated them to round after round until his money was gone. I wanted to ask the bartender why he kept taking Wendell's money if he knew it was all just a scam; instead I snatched up the laundry bag and left.

It was a chagrined dishwasher who spent his next several days off in a sulk, under tight security, being driven to and from the laundromat.

Although sullen and uncommunicative towards Red and me, behaving much like a grounded teenager, Wendell continued to work in exemplary fashion. We finally concluded that his good points for six days a week far outweighed one day of hell-raising and gave in to his pleas for freedom on his day off. Whenever he announced he was going "down town" we knew we were in for a night of it. Usually he called a taxi to get himself home. He would be dropped off at the front door of the Inn where he would ring the buzzer, forcing Red to come down and let him in. After enduring an angry tirade from his boss usually ending with, "You're fired!", Wendell would come stumbling and crying out to the kitchen where I would be waiting to see that he got upstairs in one piece, reversing Red's order issued at the front door.

Wendell paid a stiff price for his day off. His stumps would be raw and sore from the abuse they took plodding around Winchendon and thumbing a ride to the Curve Inn. He would be forced to spend several evenings sitting in the kitchen, each stump soaking in an old restaurant-size food can filled with an Epsom Salts solution.

We all endured, however, and Wendell Hadley lasted through all the years we owned the Inn. A unique little man who loved to talk big and brag about how important he was to the innkeepers.   He was so right.

VII
ON THE ROCKS WITH A TWIST

"Liquor is Quicker"

The Pub was Red's milieu during the week; both he and his domain were an attraction to all. Visitors to the Inn were all drawn to the interesting little room with its dominating chimney and fireplace, wallpaper colorfully patterned with liquor labels, and the unusual service bar copied by Al Bicknell from the English pubs. Cozy and intimate, it was easy for patrons to talk back and forth across tables, often including the bartender in the conversation. Red surprised himself by genuinely enjoying this interaction and willingly offered his opinion on any topic. To the many people who wanted to buy him a drink he always replied, "Thank you, but you can't buy the bus driver his ticket." He was really saying the State of New Hampshire would lift his liquor license if they caught him drinking while tending bar.

The Pub acted as a magnet for lovers. Red, newly hooked on human behaviour, began to consider himself astute at picking out couples conducting "les affaires d'amour". He based his judgment on two criteria: which table was selected and what drinks were ordered. In the 60's, cocktails were still the drink of choice, Martinis and Manhattans being the most popular. In Red's opinion, it was a sure sign of "hanky-panky" if a couple headed for the corner table partially hidden by the fireplace and if the gentleman ordered a potent cocktail for his date, a simple beer for himself. Ogden

Nash's, "Liquor is quicker", was one of Red's favorites to which he added his own descriptive ending, "and the third drink is a thigh opener."

If the pair stayed for a second drink, Red would peer around the open door of the Pub and, catching my eye, jerk his head toward the corner table all the while bobbing his eyebrows up and down for emphasis. I would step into the room, survey the situation and give him a smile or frown depending on whether I agreed or disagreed with his assessment.

Red spent many long hours behind the bar in the little Pub and, of all the suspected "sub rosa" situations that came under his scrutiny, three made lasting impressions.

The Pub

Dick and Eleanor

Eleanor Garth was about 35, tall, long dark hair; not too attractive. Dick Hennesy was at least ten years older, soft spoken and easy to know.

On their first visit to the Pub, they headed straight for the corner table. Red looked them over convinced they belonged in his collection. When Dick ordered two Budweisers, he had his doubts even though the couple sat holding hands for over an hour.

When their glasses were finally empty, Dick got up and walked over to the bar and asked Red if he would step into the hall with him. In a barely audible voice he said, "I've never done this before, had an affair I mean, and I'm not having much success. Perhaps she'd become interested over a sexy meal. I'd like to have a big steak, candles and a bottle of wine. Can you help me out?" His instinct confirmed, Red quickly sought me out to tell the story and explain the meal order.

Outside the March sun shone brightly. Even so, I brought a candle, place mats, napkins and silverware into the Pub and set the little corner table for a dinner meal. Earle broiled two beautiful sirloins which the waitress served along with rolls and salad. Red brought the bottle of Cabernet Sauvignon that Dick had selected. Eleanor ate all her steak and half of Dick's and, by the time they left, she was clinging to him just as he had hoped.

They returned to the Inn once a month for three years always stopping in the Pub for a glass of beer and a brief visit with Red. They ate in the dining room after that first time, always ordering steaks and wine. No candles.

In 1968, we had a note from Eleanor telling us Dick had suffered a stroke and was paralyzed. She thanked Red for his hospitality, courtesy and understanding. We never saw her again.

Joan and David

I recognized Joan Evans the minute she and David Morse walked into the Pub. Red had difficulty placing her but admitted she looked familiar. Not me! Our first meeting was clear in my memory. It was one of our orientation days at the Inn when Al Bicknell was introducing us to luncheon customers. We paused at a table in the back dining room where six women were enjoying a multi-Martini lunch. As we approached, one of the group, a gorgeous dark-haired woman jumped up and ran over to Red, linked her arm through his and said, "Who have you got here, Alfred?" "The new innkeeper and his wife, Enoch and Mary Lou Fuller," Al replied. "The new innkeeper!!" she cried, "Well, let me welcome *you* in style." Putting her arms around Red's neck she plastered her body to his and kissed him while her companions, whooping gleefully, cheered her on. Red, conservative and straight-laced as ever, calmly unwound himself and escorted the woman back to her chair saying he would look forward to seeing them *all* again. "You'll see *lots* of me, Enoch," Joan called out as another chorus of hilarity erupted from her friends.

Here she was three months later, sitting at the corner table in the Pub with a man she cheerfully introduced to Red as Dr. David Morse, her dentist! "We're married - just not to each other," she chortled. "David finished filling my tooth so I brought him out for lunch." Wealthy, spoiled and bored, Joan was aggressive and quite used to having her own way.

That first day they lingered in the Pub, going into the dining room close to the end of the serving hours. When their lunch was over, Joan asked Red if she could have a room upstairs for the afternoon. I was sorry I missed his response because I knew exactly how he felt about renting rooms by the hour. He had told me many fine places did just that to make ends meet.

They returned to the Inn regularly and each time we speculated how long the affair would last before Joan, tired of having her cavities filled, dumped the dentist. A few months later, at our New Year's Eve dinner dance, it ended more abruptly than we could have predicted. Joan, her husband and four friends had reservations. The Morses were also at the Inn that night with another group. At some point in the evening, Joan and David left their respective tables under the guise of trips to the rest rooms but instead met in the front office where Mimi and Abbie were sitting behind the desk. The Mothers told us later that Joan and Dr. Morse were locked in a passionate embrace when Joan's husband came around the corner and caught them.

Abbie charged into the Pub to get ice for the dentist's nose where Ben Evans had punched him. The Morse party departed almost immediately but Joan, brash and nervy to the end, stayed on to loudly celebrate the new year.

It was the last time we saw them and had to agree we hardly missed their business. A discovery was made some weeks after their New Year's debacle: in an antique teapot displayed on the windowsill next to the table where they always sat for lunch, were fifty tightly folded one dollar bills. "It's 'found money'," Red said wasting no time stuffing the money into his pocket. "And no less a tip than we deserved!"

Diane, Peggy and Bill

There was nothing especially remarkable about either Diane or Bill when they came into the Pub and sat at the corner table one winter afternoon. A nice looking couple in their late thirties, both were dressed for the city. He wore a brown three-piece suit; she was in a tailored wool dress. Peggy, a third in the group, joined them after a detour to the ladies' room. She was wearing a severe navy blue suit, white blouse and sensible dark oxfords.

Peggy was about forty, short and very plump. A true "5-by-5", her Dutch haircut enhanced her fat, rosy cheeks. Red, waiting to take the bar order until she was seated, was treated to a sight that was to become the focal point of the evening. As Peggy lowered her bulk into the chair, her tight skirt crept up to reveal two fat bare knees dimpling and winking over the tops of stockings rolled on 1920's garters. The combination of fashionably tailored suit, sensible shoes and pink knees was hilarious and Red had to fight down the urge to laugh. Bill caught Red's eye and glanced away in disgust.

They ordered Manhattans all around, chatting quietly among themselves. Suddenly, mid-way through a second drink, their voices rose and a serious disagreement appeared imminent. When Bill noticed Red looking over at them he got up and went to the bar. "We're arguing about our wedding. We're on our way from Boston to Wilmington, Vermont to make arrangements to be married there next week, but I want to be married right here - *tonight!* The girls are giving me a hard time. What do you think?"

Red was taken aback. How could he make wedding plans for people he didn't know? He shrewdly advised, "How about having dinner first? After a good meal you'll be in a better position to decide." "No!" Bill exclaimed. "There *must* be a Justice of the Peace in town that could marry us tonight. Perhaps in your parlour." Red agreed to call Webb Sherman, the Town Clerk, and see if he could come over, but only if Bill and the two ladies would have dinner first. Finally they agreed. Bill and Diane walked into the dining room together, with Peggy bringing up a considerable rear.

Meanwhile Red telephoned Webb. "I'm just getting into the bath tub, Enoch," was his answer. "Can it wait?" "No Webb, it can't," Red insisted. "Take your bath, then please come to the Inn."

After they had eaten, the trio returned to the Pub for a liqueur. Bill immediately asked Red if the wedding was on or not. "I've got the license and the blood tests. There's just one thing; I want the word 'obey' put back in the ceremony."

Red was not convinced this was all legitimate but, when Webb arrived and looked things over, he declared the papers were in order. Red told him Bill wanted "obey" rather than "cherish" and, there being nothing else to prevent his wedding from taking place, Bill asked Red to stand up with him.

The wedding party made their way to the parlour. There, directed by Webb, Bill took his position with Red on his right. Then the bride was asked to move up; Peggy stepped into the designated spot next to Bill. In Red's mind she was an inconceivable bride and he reacted by reaching across in front of the groom to move her out of the way. Red thought no one could be crazy enough to marry plump Peggy with the rolled stockings, when Diane seemed to be such a perfect choice. Bill's arm shot out, blocking Red and preventing any further disruption. The wedding commenced; "obey" slipped smoothly into place and the bride promised without hesitation.

I was watching the ceremony from the parlour doorway and was suddenly aware Webb had stopped speaking and was signalling to me. Bill had forgotten a ring! With the wedding on hold, I climbed on a Pub chair, removed one of the brass rings from the cafe curtains and delivered it to Webb.

As soon as the last official word was intoned, even before he kissed the bride, Bill turned to Peggy and put a hand on each of her shoulders. Towering over her, he gazed down into her eyes and said, "You promised to obey and I am now ordering you to never wear rolled stockings again." The bride beamed up at her husband and nodded her head.

They departed the next morning and only those in the know were aware that the plump hand waving goodbye so happily was adorned with our brass curtain ring.

Last Call

Business in the Pub was in its ascendancy during the 1960's. New Hampshire had relaxed some of its liquor laws and table hopping with drink in hand was now allowed as long as it was all done in one room. Carrying a drink from Pub to dining room was still not permitted except by our bartenders and waitresses.

The Pub saw the birth of the *Troy-Fitzwilliam Lions Club*. Eric Wentworth, a Tail-Twister extraordinaire, roared through the assembled members who packed the little room once a month before adjourning to the back dining room for their dinner meeting.

The Fitzwilliam Conference, the prestigious annual gathering of college and preparatory school admissions officers, grew from a casual discussion between Red and two officials from Worcester Polytech, Ken Nourse and Bill Elliott. A chance stop for a cocktail and lunch, combined with the interest and salesmanship of the innkeeper, led to the first conference in 1969. A large group was expected and when Red was asked how many the Inn could sleep, he quickly replied, "It depends on how friendly they are!" The fifty-plus, in 1969, were the foundation of what was to become a conference of international scope.

In summer the Pub was crowded every night. Guests staying in the Inn, or those coming in just for dinner, would have cocktails before they ate and reconvene afterwards for a nightcap.

By law, Red could serve liquor until one a.m. Monday through Friday; midnight on Saturday night and eight p.m. on Sunday. New Hampshire liquor licenses held Sundays from twelve midnight to twelve noon sacrosanct and no alcoholic beverages could be served except in private clubs or by special permission. Friday nights were apt to be raucous, but usually Red was able to bring things to a close without a problem. Occasionally he ran into a disagreeable type who wanted more to drink, but only once do I remember the police coming at Red's request to remove an especially nasty customer.

Mimi, whose room was directly over the Pub, was often disturbed by the bursts of laughter and catcalls that shot up through her floorboards. On

particularly boisterous nights she would grab her shoe and pound on the floor in front of the closet right above where Red stood behind the bar. No one else could hear her signal, but *he* knew his mother-in-law was issuing her own "Last Call".

VIII
FOOD FOR THE HUNGRY

"Company's Coming!"

There were days when the front hall of the Inn, as well as the narrow entrance to the dining room, resembled the end of a cattle drive: hungry guests, panicked that they would not get fed, massed in wild-eyed confusion. It would have been much less hair-raising if we had run our dining room on a "reservations only" basis, but Red was determined to squeeze in all comers. If I complained about the chaos created by this philosophy, I would be admonished with the quote, "an inn provides rest for the weary, drink for the thirsty and food for the hungry". Then for emphasis he would add, "And not *just* those who think to call ahead!" I realized this was true, but I knew my husband and, although he never expected to get rich as an innkeeper, he was a thrifty Yankee and to let dollars walk out the door because there was no place for them to sit, would be tantamount to renouncing his heritage.

To put an extra burden on one's wife was one thing, to push a chef to the extreme was quite another. Red's commitment to take in all who stopped for a meal would never have succeeded with any chef other than Earle Aaskov. Always innovative and flexible in the kitchen, he was willing and able to roll with the unexpected when having to make fast substitutions if an entree ran out. At first, without past records of meals served, this was a calculated risk we had to take. As Red meticulously built his own historical data, the numbers of people Earle prepared for became more accurate.

Weekdays we drew our trade from the small towns around Mt. Monadnock, plus the cities of Keene, New Hampshire; Winchendon and Gardner, Massachusetts. These were primarily parties on social outings, but the Inn was also a popular gathering place for business lunches. Salespeople and executives spent time and money in the Pub, before they adjourned to the dining room; a fact that delighted the innkeeper.

On weekends, patrons journeyed from a greater distance, especially when Red's whereabouts became known to former customers and friends. They thought nothing of driving over from Vermont, down from northern New Hampshire and up from Boston, Providence and all points in between. It was a wonderful tribute to his hospitality.

If we found that a dining room guest was celebrating a birthday, a special cake with candles would be delivered to the table. The waitresses and I gathered to sing "Happy Birthday" accompanied by Red on the upright piano. He loved these occasions and would leave whatever he was doing to add his personal touch to the festivities.

Earle's delectable meals began bringing in new and repeat business. This was particularly gratifying since word-of-mouth was our only means of advertising. The menu always featured Roast Prime Rib of Beef on Saturday night and Roast Leg of Lamb on Sunday noon. The latter was prepared with bits of garlic inserted under the skin before cooking. Each week a glorious aroma filled the air throughout Fitzwilliam center, tantalizing residents and churchgoers.

Of particular popularity, at both lunch and dinner, were our small loaves of pumpkin bread served on individual bread boards. Abbie had purloined the recipe from the baker at one of Red's prior managerial posts and passed it on to Earle. The bread made such a hit with our guests that Mimi sold

The main dining room

loaves in Fulla Gifts as well.

As hostess, my station was at the dining room entrance and, on more hectic days, I resembled an overwrought cowhand at a roundup. It was up to me to make order out of the milling crowd, make small talk with those I recognized and generally set a tone of welcome. If it was someone's first visit to the Inn I asked, "Had you called ahead to tell us you were coming?" This seemed less onerous than "Do you have a reservation?" which Red considered too much like asking for a password. The question also served to plant the seed that, in the future, prior warning of their arrival would be helpful. If there had been no advanced call, I would try to fit them in, often stretching our dining room capacity.

Frequently I would have to ask the overflow to wait in the Pub or one of the front rooms until a table was available. I became quite adept at keeping everyone content. Sometimes this was confirmed by a departing customer with the comment, "You make innkeeping look like such fun!" Red would raise his eyebrows and peer at me over his glasses with a look that said, "Aren't you ashamed for getting upset by a 'little' business?"

Sunday nights we served a buffet supper. The configuration of the back dining room was altered to set up banquet tables on which Earle amassed an array of salads and hot dishes, including seafood Newburg and roast beef, home-baked breads and desserts. The meal was an easy one to serve since the waitresses only took beverage orders and cleared tables; the guests did all the heavy work by serving themselves from the buffet.

Monday's noon meal was a smaller version of the Sunday buffet. It was Earle's day off and Bob would replace the Newburg and beef with less costly items such as American Chop Suey and baked beans with ham.

The Munroes

When Jasper and Ernestine Munroe, a retired couple from Jaffrey, discovered the buffet they appeared every Sunday evening just as the dining room opened. Their punctuality was unerring and we joked about not seating anyone else until the Munroes were in position at the "starting gate". They would make a dash for a corner table. Ernestine always sat with her back to the wall with Jasper opposite her where he could command a view of the buffet.

The third Sunday of their patronage, one of the waitresses came to Red with an astounding observation, "I think Mrs. Munroe is filling her pocketbook with seafood Newburg". It was too startling to believe: Newburg was so messy. Nevertheless, we both kept an eye on the Munroes, patrolling the table, filling water glasses and pausing to chat. They were extremely clever and, if it had not been that Ernestine was built like a bird, not weighing more than 85 pounds, we would have been convinced she was consuming the Newburg at the table.

As the weeks passed Red became increasingly disturbed over the situation, particularly after he overheard Jasper directing Ernestine to "Take roast beef this week, we have enough Newburg." What a quandry! It was supposed to be an "all you can eat buffet" but Jasper was selecting their groceries for the *week!* Then, to make matters worse they began showing up on Monday noons. Now the pocketbook was "fed" American Chop Suey, beans, ham and brown bread.

More than a month went by until one Monday Ernestine slipped up. She stepped to the buffet while Jasper was in the men's room and made the mistake of leaving her pocketbook agape on the chair, not realizing Red was positioned just right to get a look at its contents. There was our food, neatly organized in narrow plastic boxes. His quick assessment was that her bag had been cleverly designed and outfitted for its unique role in life; the Munroes were into big-time poaching.

Red made a decision on the spot and wrote out a dining room check for three buffet luncheons for the Munroe party of two. When Jasper and Ernestine came out of the dining room, Red handed Jasper the check. As expected, it evoked the comment, "I believe there's a mistake; this is for *three* luncheons." "No mistake, Mr. Munroe," Red replied. "The third charge is for the one in Mrs. Munroe's pocketbook." Maintaining his composure, Jasper paid the additional price and, taking Ernestine's elbow, swept from the Inn without so much as an apology.

We were sure it was the last we would see of them; but a year later they arrived on a day when lunch was being served from the menu. Ernestine

carried a package which she handed to me. It contained an exquisite covered Limoge cheese plate. With a slight bow, Jasper presented Red with a series of eight Currier and Ives hunting scenes, the riders' bright red coats standing out against the sepia tones associated with the artist's work. Both gifts became permanent and endearing reminders of an unbelievable saga.

E. Nock

In the 1960's, Fitzwilliam "society" was principally those of retirement age. The town had a cross-section of U.S. Navy, Army, Marine and Air Force officers who, by some subliminal means, had gotten word that the town was a haven for forgetting war and violence. These retirees were in residence from May to October and then fled to Florida or Arizona.

Betty Brown was the leader of these geriatric jet-setters, claiming her status on the grounds that she had been Queen of the Mardi Gras in the 1930's and that her husband, a retired general, outranked those of her peers.

Betty, her husband and their friends came into the Inn often for dinner. She would phone us to announce their arrival and request her favorite table, just inside the dining room.

Once seated, she would call out her bar order in the direction of the Pub where she knew the innkeeper waited to hear from her. It was a familiar routine. Betty refused to use the diminutive, "Red", preferring his given name pronounced ENIK. However, when her Southern drawl rang out it was, "E. Nock, I'll have an extra dry Mahtini," always followed by, "and this time, E. Nock, put some gin in it!"

Patrons in the dining room snapped to attention; those in the Pub watched to see Red's reaction. With a magician's flourish and a completely straight face he placed a cocktail shaker on top of the bar for all to see, a small amount of crushed ice in the bottom. Over this he poured three carefully measured ounces of Beefeaters Gin which he stirred ever so gently "to keep it from bruising," he explained. Taking a frosted glass from the ice, he strained the drink into it and selected an olive which he dropped into the cold gin. His final act was to take the *unopened* bottle of Nouilly Pratt Dry Vermouth and ceremoniously pass it over the glass.

When the drink was served, everyone waited for Betty to take her first sip. Her voice soon rang out again, "You're getting better at it, E. Nock, but it still needs less vermouth." A burst of hysterics exploded from the Pub and the innkeeper was sure he had had the last laugh. Or had he?

Bettina, Betty's daughter from her first marriage, had been a bridesmaid for Grace Kelly when she married the Prince of Monaco. On a busy summer day, Betty telephoned the Inn and spoke to Mimi. "Tell E. Nock I'm sending over two very important friends. He's to give them special treatment." The dining room was crowded; I had taken the day off and Red was doing double-duty in the Pub and dining room.

At 3 p.m. Betty phoned again. Red answered this time. Her deep drawl rolled over the line, "What did you think of *them,* E. Nock?" "Think of who, Betty?" "Why, Grace and the Prince, of course. They stopped to see me on their way to visit one of the children at camp. They asked about a decent luncheon place and naturally I sent them to you." Red refused to believe that two such well-known celebrities had come into *his* dining room, been served by *his* waitresses and gone out without being recognized. Mimi and Abbie were just as dumbfounded. The two elderly ladies simultaneously remembered their favorite information source and hurried to the Guest Book. Stunned, they held out the book for Red to see the signature, *"Grace Kelly Grimaldi, Monaco"*. The innkeeper was not laughing.

A Fan on the Edge

Without a doubt we missed other celebrities who sought the peace and anonymity offered by our country setting. In our defense I must say that we were not "up" on *prime time* television shows and never went to movies. We worked when most people played. And, unbelievable as it may seem, unless a celebrity was introduced by others in their party, we remained focused on giving the same courtesy, comfort and good service to everyone.

Because Red's schedule gave him time off during the afternoon, that became his hour to view television. He had become hooked on the mystery/soap opera "The Edge of Night" and woe be to anything standing in the way of this program. One of Red's favorite characters was a lawyer whose name in the show was "Phil Capece".

It was this unwitting actor who, with his wife, children and another family stopped for dinner one winter evening. Bound for Vermont, they had been lured to the Inn by our billboard on Route 12. The dining room was crowded and these folks had no reservation, but by pushing together four small tables, I was able to accommodate them in the center of the front dining room.

Red was helping in the dining room pouring water and bussing trays. Unfortunately for "Phil Capece", as Red approached their table, he recognized his hero from "The Edge of Night". He descended on the unsuspecting soap star with open arms, broad grin and white eyebrows bouncing. He grasped "Capece" by the hand and yanked him to his feet exclaiming, "You're Phil Capece! You're Phil Capece!" Furiously pumping the man's arm up and down he turned to draw in the entire dining room, raised his voice and announced enthusiastically, "It's Phil Capece from 'The Edge of Night'!"

The silence that greeted him made it obvious that no one had heard of "Phil Capece" or the program but, in response to the innkeeper's obvious delirium, they nodded politely before resuming their dinner conversations. "Capece" rallied first, graciously acknowledged his exuberant fan and introduced him to his family and friends before returning to his dinner.

Every time Red passed through the dining room he would glance over at the table just to be sure it was not a dream that "Phil Capece" was actually eating in *his* dining room, in *his* Inn. I was glad he missed hearing one of the "Capece" children say to his father, "Who *was* that funny man, Daddy?"

Holidays

Mother's Day was our biggest day of the year; followed by Thanksgiving and Easter. We served close to 300 each Mother's Day. Red's explanation for this phenomenon was, "What else can one do for mother but get her out of the kitchen for the day, and because no one else wants to cook, restaurants are the beneficiaries."

We always had three dining room sittings on these special holidays: noon, 1:30 p.m. and 3 p.m. Such occasions necessitated more elaborate reservation charts which I would draw up for each seating, plotting the table bookings accordingly.

Although Red believed in feeding everyone who showed up, he was adamant about honoring reservations and woe to me if a party had to wait any longer than just the time it took to prepare their table.

We never had a printed menu on big holidays. Instead the entree choices would be announced by the waitress. To make it easy on everyone, guests and management alike, there was one price for the meal regardless of entree.

Lobster Bisque or Fruit Cup

Tossed Salad   Home Baked Bread

Roast Lamb

Roast Prime Rib

Seafood Newburg

Homemade Desserts   Beverage

Roast Turkey would be substituted for the Roast Lamb on Thanksgiving and Roast Duckling on Easter. We always had crackers and relish tray, nut cups, special juice or cider on the table beforehand.

At the height of Mother's Day service, with a crowd of walk-ins milling about in the ante-rooms, the dining rooms filled to absolute capacity and then some, Red would appear in the entrance way and beam with pride at the sea of faces, all chewing in unison, and bask in the knowledge that *his* Inn was the setting for this beautiful band of "Munching Mommas".

It was enough to make an innkeeper's cash register burst with satisfaction!

A Blizzard of Turkey

As a rule a little rain, snow or fog never intruded on the success of holiday business; that is until the Thanksgiving of 1969. We had been blessed with a bumper crop of 250 reservations, and thanks to Red's historical data, he and Earle knew to a bird how many turkeys to order.

For several days ahead of Thanksgiving, delectable aromas drifted from the kitchen as Earle pre-roasted the turkeys. He prepared the dressing separately and baked it in adjacent ovens. The day before the holiday, the turkeys would be "stripped" into piles of white and dark meat. Then, using an ice cream scoop for portion control, servings of dressing were placed in shallow pans; pre-weighed assortments of meat laid on top. A cloth was spread over the servings, turkey broth ladled liberally throughout and the pans moved to the walk-in box. The servings would be heated the next morning and "gravied" as orders were called for by the waitresses.

We woke Thanksgiving morning to a blizzard. Snow was drifting and blowing so fast plowing and shoveling were a losing battle. We had known bad weather was predicted, but there had been no hint of what we were seeing.

The phones began to ring about 10 a.m. and gradually throughout the morning all but a handful of customers had cancelled, apologizing profusely, but nonetheless cancelling.

Holiday house guests were usually in the area to have Thanksgiving at the home of family or friends. Some of these ended up Inn captives and at noontime we fed them and about 15 walk-ins; that was it for the day. Red kept on a skeleton staff of those who lived in town and sent Earle and everyone else home.

That evening we had some travelers seeking haven from the storm so quite a few additional rooms were taken unexpectedly. We put out cold turkey and sandwich bread for everyone but barely a dent was made in the tower of turkey that greeted us everywhere we turned.

Hot and Cold Turkey Sandwiches and Turkey Pot Pies, were on the menus for a week; all abundantly laced with light and dark meat.

The South Pond Menace

Our first year we were amazed to discover that the number of Fitzwilliam residents began increasing around Memorial Day as the "snowbirds" who had flown to Florida and Arizona for the winter all returned to roost. By July 4th the population had almost tripled, mainly due to the influx of "summer people" and vacationers at Laurel Lake.

There were also two private youth camps on the lake - Fleur de Lis and South Pond Cabins. Philosophically the camps were basically the same: address the needs of the whole child through the teaching of camping and waterfront skills to develop self-reliance and self-discipline. Guidance in interpersonal skills was also a part of the philosophy.

There were two visiting days for parents, each on a Sunday in July and August. It was at this point that the philosophies of the two camps diverged.

Frances Beede, Director of Fleur de Lis, strongly discouraged parents from taking their daughters off camp property during visitations. Instead, Miss Beede offered several options: those wishing to attend the Saturday evening campfire could either stay at the Inn or rent an extra room on the second floor of camp headquarters. Many parents commuted to camp for the day on Sunday, bringing sumptuous picnics to share with their daughter.

The Putnams, who ran South Pond Cabins, placed no restrictions on the boys leaving the camp with their families. As there was no space at South Pond for parents to stay overnight, we inherited them.

Red and I were not prepared that first summer for the South Pond parents. They were a special breed; a blend of money, private schools, private planes, extra dry Martinis, perfect Manhattans and LaCoste clothes.

It quickly became apparent that visiting their sons was secondary to gathering in the Pub, renewing acquaintances with other parents and comparing notes on the upgrading of lives and jobs. The babble rose a few decibels with each olive or cherry that disappeared at the end of a cocktail.

Meanwhile, relationships with each other at a new high, the boys, ignored and unsupervised, were in and out of the pool shouting and laughing as they savored their freedom. All thoughts of self-reliance and self-discipline were lost as they succumbed to the pleasure of being released from camp rules.

Red was behind the bar his face running with perspiration, eyeglasses at their usual half-mast position as he rushed to keep up with the drink orders from dining room and Pub.

About 6:30 p.m. Mrs. Putnam phoned the Inn to tell us she needed the boys back at camp by 8 p.m. for campfire and "Didn't we know enough not to detain the parents and children?" I went to each group in the Pub and relayed the message. Some of the parents responded, retrieved their boys and made it to the dining room by 7 p.m. Others remained fixed in their chairs; the loud talk went on and the activity around the pool continued unchecked.

Suddenly there was a loud report. "Small caliber cannon", was my first thought. It came from the patio area adjacent to the pool. Red must have had the same thought as he brushed by me at top speed covering the distance from Pub to pool in record time.

He found that the boys, bored with conventional shuffleboard, had created their own version which involved throwing the disks off the diving board into the water. One of the disks had been thrown with such force it had smashed through the roof of the patio falling onto the flagstone floor.

That was enough for Red who made an equally rapid return trip to the Pub and ordered the remaining parents to collect their off-spring. He described the mayhem that had been created.

Immediately out came the check books accompanied by offers to pay for the damages. "The cost will be reflected on your room accounts," Red told them. At this point he was so angry I was greatly relieved when the parents finally left.

All Around the Mountain
During the 1960's, good eating places in the Monadnock region were few and far between. Red felt it was to his advantage to check them out and get acquainted with other innkeepers.

When we were able to take an evening off, we would eat at other establishments. This should have been relaxing, but Red would start by finding fault with the lack of aesthetic arrangement of the food on his plate, repeating one of his adages that "people eat with their eyes". Then he would count the burned out bulbs in the chandeliers and look askance at spotted glasses or silverware. At the end of the evening, we were both so unnerved it was a relief to get back to Fitzwilliam.

The Dublin Inn

Anna Yost's Dublin Inn, in Red's professional opinion, was the finest eating place in the entire area. He never viewed it as competition, believing it was in a class by itself in service, atmosphere, quality and variety of menu choices and the dining room appointments of table linens, sterling silver, crystal and fine china.

If we chose to entertain any house guests who had booked with us for an extended time, we always took them to the Dublin Inn for dinner.

Anna's career in the restaurant business began in New Jersey and when she came to Dublin she brought her cook, Franz Berger. He eventually left Dublin and re-opened the Old Forge in Rindge.

The Inn at East Hill Farm

Parker Whitcomb owned and operated this wonderful family resort in Troy. Here Red could relax on a night out in an atmosphere completely different from his Inn. East Hill Farm offered square dance weekends and, for families, there was skiing, skating and sleigh rides in winter and the pool and horseback riding in summer: a tremendously popular and unique facility.

Parker was also a UNH Hotel School graduate and, of all Red's associates in the Monadnock region, was the most constant sounding-board and loyal friend.

Woodbound Inn

Ed and Peg Brummer had made a huge success of Woodbound, a summer resort in Rindge. They also took transients in the dining room.

Ed was president of the New Hampshire Hotel Association and extremely well respected in the industry. He was also active in the Monadnock Region Association and encouraged Red to attend meetings where he could exchange ideas with others involved in tourism.

Winding Brook Lodge

This was a "state of the art" motel with an elegant formal dining room boasting the first salad bar in the area. The manager, Frank Power, was a friend of Red's from his Early American Inn days. He was an older no-nonsense hotel man; strait-laced and formal, never appearing in other than a three-piece suit. He ran a "tight ship" while at the same time exuding charm and solicitude throughout his establishment.

The Black Lantern

Hector Dionne was owner, operator and chef of the Black Lantern Restaurant on Route 12 in Swanzey. Our two establishments were different: one was operated by a flamboyant Frenchman, the other an ultra-conservative New Englander.

Hector did not believe in reservations and instilled in his waitresses the need to get customers in and out of the restaurant in one hour, tops. He could afford to be a little "pushy"; his place was popular, with long lines of people waiting to be seated. Red was secretly envious of Hector's success.

Red achieved great satisfaction when it was discovered that two of Hector's cooks were coming to our Monday noon buffet for Earle's Swedish meatballs. A Fitzwilliam resident, also one of Hector's waitresses, confided that Hector had heard how good they were and was trying to duplicate the recipe from the taste described by his henchmen. Red was delighted when it was reported back that their experiments had all failed.

Red always viewed competition as healthy. "It keeps us on our toes," he would say to me. And there were certainly days when providing food for the hungry overworked *my* toes!

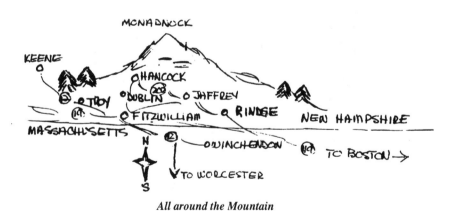

All around the Mountain

*The innkeeper and the apprentice
at dining room "command table"*

*Abbie in the Pub
(original cooking fireplace with oven door)*

THE KEY
The Innkeeper's Symbol

IX
BANQUETS, BUSES AND BRIDES

Trapped by Space

In our second year, we began to get more inquiries from tour companies and organizations wanting to book banquets and conferences, as well as bridal couples looking for space for wedding receptions.

However, the Inn's dining rooms only held 100 people. If we used this space for banquets, there would be no room to feed transients or house guests. Nor could we offer a place for dancing, often requested when party arrangements were being made.

Privacy was an added problem: no one wanted to conduct a meeting or open shower gifts in the midst of a dining room filled with people who were not part of the function. This very situation caused Red great embarrassment when Dr. Carleton Smith, an attendee at one of the Troy-Fitzwilliam Lions' Club dinner meetings, shouted at him for clattering through the back dining room where the club was seated. "Don't you know enough to have rubber heels on those shoes? Banging through here on leather heels is thoughtless and rude."

Often we had to turn people away because our facilities were not adequate. This nagged at Red and he was determined to correct the situation in order to get some of the lucrative banquet revenue.

The Sullivan Wedding

The Sullivan wedding alerted us to the extreme urgency for additional space. Scheduled for 50 people with a full "sit-down" meal, we needed all our ingenuity to rearrange the front dining room and comfortably seat the reception guests. Banquet tables were used where possible.

Our *regular* noon meal would be served in the back dining room. Transient patrons would be directed to enter through the patio in order not to intrude on the reception.

The wedding was at 10 a.m. in Winchendon and the guests began arriving at the Inn about noon, and they kept coming until it became apparent that at least 75 people were trying to crowd into the spaces set for 50. Clearly, the Sullivans had booked incorrectly. The overflow had to be seated in the back dining room using tables designated for transients.

We were fortunate that Earle was able to put together the extra meals. He always prepared for a percentage over the confirmed number and with his ability to improvise, we got through the crisis.

I am sure my body developed an immediate anxious twitch when Red dashed by exclaiming, "Quick! Set up all available card tables in the front parlour for the transient lunch people." When I suggested closing the Inn for just that meal, he looked over his glasses at me and said sternly, "Nothing doing. We're *open.*"

Food service for the reception began promptly and at the same time our parlour tables began to fill up. To my chagrin, no one minded sitting at a card table. "The parlour is so charming," was the reply each time I explained the situation.

By now the staff was involved in serving the reception so I stepped in as the parlour waitress. I took the orders and had all I could do to make my way to the kitchen through the dining room crowds where the wedding guests were happily table-hopping.

"How can I get back through here with a loaded tray?" I asked Red. In all seriousness he replied, "As I see it you have three choices." He was so quick with an answer when it came to making money that I should have known what was coming. "You can carry the trays up and down Richmond Road from the kitchen; or carry them up the front stairs, down the hall to the back kitchen stairs; or go out the front door, across the north lawn and around the swimming pool. Take your pick."

Certain that I would get run over on Richmond Road and equally sure the flights of steps would be just as treacherous, I chose the north lawn route. The experience was worse than anything I had been called on to do as part of the innkeeping team; but Red was delighted with the arrangement and between drink orders he would catch sight of me with my tray held high, going across the lawn and disappearing behind the fence that enclosed the pool.

As I cleared my tables, the last tray was my Waterloo; my own fault for loading it too full. I made it as far as the outside kitchen door when my arm suddenly began to shake. The tray tilted, dishes shifted and the load crashed down in the midst of the garbage barrels.

It was time to add a banquet room.

The Patio Room

Ruth Hutchinson, an interior designer to the hotel industry and a friend of Red's, was glad to come up and give us advice in return for dinner and a room for the night. We particularly wanted her opinion on turning the patio into a year-round dining room.

"Enoch," she began after her examination of the patio, "the room cries out for 'tur-quaz' and white." And so, based on all her recommendations, we purchased tables and chairs to accommodate 100. The chairs were light-weight metal with straps of plastic forming the seats and backs: 50 white and 50 turquoise. Because the stone flooring presented too risky a challenge for regular china and glassware, we purchased plastic glasses and the best quality Melmac service.

Interchangeable screens and windows were installed. For summer, we hung sheer white curtains; for the winter I made heavier drapes.

At first we heated the room with a wood stove which proved to be less than effective: guests complained strenuously about the cold stone floor. Eventually we installed electric baseboard heat and were forced to cover the beautiful flagstones with a false wooden floor on which we laid carpet squares.

Buses

With the completion of the Patio banquet room, Red's enthusiasm for drawing large groups knew no bounds. Bus tours were the first to book with us. These were very profitable and, with Red timing everything right, we were able to accommodate two tour groups: the first at 11 a.m., the second at 1 p.m., two buses each. This was *four* buses in one day. Halleluia!

As we had only enough service for one group of 100 (the bus groups usually totalled 90), the clearing, dishwashing and re-setting was an enormous task. "But, we got through it," Red would chortle with glee. "There's nothing better for my morale than watching 100 people munch and gulp in *my* banquet room!"

The Patio was worked overtime in the fall when foliage tours and camera clubs were almost a daily occurrence. Some of the smaller clubs stayed overnight, touring the area during the day and returning to the Inn late in the afternoon. These were booked by a tour company in New Jersey and we were delighted to see them come year after year: nice people and great business. We offered a package price including lunch, dinner, room and breakfast. They spent evenings in the Pub. Another plus!

One day about 2:30 p.m., when the fourth bus had just disappeared out of town, a distraught man clutching a uniform cap came into the dining room and made an astounding request. "I have a bus load of senior citizens outside. Somehow our original lunch arrangements got fouled up. I've stopped at every restaurant all the way over through Hinsdale, Winchester and Richmond. No luck anywhere! At least they were allowed to use the rest rooms. I can't expect this group to ride all the way back to Boston on an empty stomach. Can you give us anything?" I knew by the flicker of interest in Red's eyes what would happen next. "We *could* probably make sandwiches and coffee for them. Sure, bring them on in," he said. Earle had left for the afternoon so the Mothers and I went to the kitchen and put together platters of peanut butter sandwiches while Red made the coffee. They expressed such gratitude and over-paid so much for the meager fare that I felt guilty for wanting to turn them away.

Money Grows On Trees
October became our single busiest month simply because of the sight-seers attracted by fall foliage. Tours, transient lunch business and house guests flocked to the Inn and often booked their space for the following year as they checked out.

The staff, the Mothers and I would be exhausted during this time, and, to our distress, the overworked plumbing produced more encounters with "a horse in the ladies' room".

Even Red, who usually appeared tireless even in the face of his diabetic condition remarked, "I think it's time to go out and shake the trees and get all the leaves off." Then he would immediately counter that with, "Next month when there's no one around I'll want to go out and glue them all back on."

Banquets
With our added space, companies who wanted to arrange small conferences would arrive late on a Sunday afternoon and stay at least two days. Off-season this was wonderful use of a facility that might otherwise be empty. The Patio was a perfect venue for both meals and meetings. Our guest rooms, often unused during "down" times, would be mostly full. The Pub business also benefited as the groups unwound there before and after dinner.

Hector
We were able to do some Christmas party business also. On quiet winter evenings, when regular dining room trade was at a minimum, we could feed groups in the Patio and use the back dining room for dancing. Ordinarily, because we had a piano available, groups would bring in a pianist and bass player or a couple of guitarists.

Christmas parties were important and enabled us to build a little financial cushion to see us over the lean winter months. One such party was booked by Hector Dionne for his Black Lantern staff. He wanted a bar set up on the Patio and chose our "full" buffet with roast beef. "And some of those Swedish meatballs," he added with a wink.

They made it a gala evening. No group knows how to party as well as people normally in the business of serving others. Their laughter, gaiety and general party hoopla could be heard all the way out to the Pub.

Fortunately the dining rooms were sparsely filled on this December evening because suddenly Hector burst through from the Patio in the throes of a wild tango with one of his staff. As he pirouetted through the tables, his pants suddenly dropped to his ankles causing him to fall down; at once exposing his Santa Claus undershorts.

We were in hysterics as we watched him crawl off on his hands and knees. Red, ever conservative, chased after him to help restore his dignity never considering the flamboyant Frenchman probably devised the trick on purpose.

Mr. Governor

The Cheshire County Republican Women's Club sponsored an annual dinner dance and, once we had the proper space, they booked one of their soirees with us.

Walter Peterson was the Governor of New Hampshire at this time and it was widely advertised that he and his wife, Dorothy, would be in attendance.

Everyone was dressed in formal attire; a truly glittering assembly. After dinner the dancing began in the back dining room. The governor and his wife started it off, dancing alone for the first number. Unexpectedly, there was suddenly a third person on the dance floor. He moved in perfect time to their steps, his arms slightly raised from his sides forming a wide circle around the first couple. The badges and insignia on his uniform caught the light in competition with Dorothy's jewelry. It was the New Hampshire State Trooper assigned to guard the governor taking his job very seriously.

Brides

Wedding receptions were one of the most satisfying events: it was a thrilling occasion for the bride and groom, their families and throng of guests.

There were times when both wedding and reception were held at the Inn. Webb Sherman would come over and perform the ceremony in the parlour. These usually were small in scale; but none smaller than that of the couple who arrived on the bus and announced their intentions to marry. The 60's were a time when young people did everything in defiance of the norm, so we were not surprised. Webb officiated, Red and I served as witnesses.

Webb had barely closed his book when the bride and groom disappeared out the door and hurried off up the Upper Troy Road towards Bowkerville. They returned an hour or so later, slightly disheveled with a few bits of grass and dirt clinging to their hair and clothes. They thanked us for a lovely time and took off for the bus stop.

Each Maloney daughter was also married in the parlour. The oldest, a decorator, had seen a photo of the Inn parlour in a Better Homes and Gardens book on interior design and picked this as the room in which she wanted to be married. The family was from Texas, but that did not stop them: all the wedding arrangements were made by telephone or mail!

The wedding party and guests flew in to Boston, rented cars and drove to the Inn; 30 people in all. They stayed from Friday to Monday and had a wonderful time.

Our self-esteem as innkeepers was certainly inflated when, three years later, another wedding was planned for the second daughter and the entire entourage returned.

Front Parlour, site of many weddings
(portrait of Earle Fitzwilliam over divan)

The Daley Wedding

Marcia Daley and her fiancé were to be married in August. Accompanied by Mrs. Daley, they stopped in several times making detailed arrangements concerning menu and seating. Mrs. Daley intended to do the flowers for the head table herself and for each guest table she planned nosegay centerpieces.

The ceremony took place at the Cathedral of the Pines and, when the bride and her attendants arrived at the Inn, we were struck by the elegance of their gowns. Mrs. Daley and the groom's mother also wore long dresses; the men were in tuxedos.

The reception was in full swing by 1 p.m. and we could hear toasts being offered to the bridal couple. Either Red or I would make periodic trips to the Patio to check on the proceedings. We were gratified to see the flock of happy faces.

At 2 p.m. the dining room was still busy. Red and I stood in the hallway by the Pub waiting to cash-out any departing customers. Just then Mr. Daley, accompanied by his son, walked through from the Patio.

Mr. Daley was over 6 feet tall, but as they approached it was clear he was walking heavily, his shoulders bowed. As they drew even with us we saw that the color was draining from his face. His son said, "Dad's not feeling well."

They rounded the corner into the men's room and minutes later the building shook with a sickening crash. Young McPhee rushed from the men's room saying, "My father has collapsed. I think he's had a heart attack. Please get a doctor right away!"

Bob Berry, trained in CPR, took the boy by the arm and both went into the men's room. While I raced to the telephone, Red took the stairs two-at-a-time to alert Dr. and Mrs. Inkster, guests at the Inn, and ask if they could come down and help.

The first call I made was to the Fitzwilliam Rescue Squad, then I tried to reach Drs. Smith and McMaster, both of whom lived in town. They were unavailable.

Harry Inkster arrived, took one look at Mr. Daley and shook his head. "I can't administer any medication because I'm not licensed in New Hampshire. The rescue squad is your best bet; but I think he was gone before he hit the floor."

The rescue squad, all volunteers connected to the fire department, arrived almost immediately. They began resuscitation attempts, but to no avail. Sadly, with no physician in attendance, it was necessary to call the Keene ambulance to move Mr. Daley's body to the hospital where he could be officially pronounced dead.

Meanwhile, the wedding reception continued at full tilt on the Patio. The Daley boy had no idea how to break the news to his mother and sisters, one of whom was the bride!

The question of what to do about Mrs. Daley was resolved when she came out looking for her husband. Evelyn and Harry Inkster took her into the library, closed the doors and broke the news. Red decided to at least inform the groom and had one of the waitresses ask him to come in from the reception. The distressed young man was instantly torn between telling his bride, or allowing her a few more minutes of blissful ignorance until after they had cut the wedding cake. He opted for the latter choice.

We called on all our emotional strength as we dealt with the devastation and grief going on in the library and then assumed another demeanor to go and check the reception. The bride had been told that her father was not feeling well and that her mother had taken him home.

Yet another macabre discovery was made when the ambulance arrived: the configuration of the men's room prevented removal of the body on a stretcher in the conventional manner. "We'll have to stand him up and walk him out. There's just no other way," the attendants told Red.

"Good God!" I said, "How do we keep the dining room customers from seeing this take place?"

"We'll put a screen across the hallway," Red decided, "and ask people to wait a few minutes, that's all. It's the bride and the wedding guests I'm most concerned about. You stay in the back dining room and divert anyone going to the restrooms to the upstairs baths. Make up some reason, like the plumbing isn't working."

Eventually the situation played itself out: Mr. Daley was taken to the hospital; the son, his mother and sisters went home and, once the cake was cut, the groom took his bride out the back way to the parking lot. Ironically, they were forced to make the trip in a wildly decorated car, back to the house she had left so happily that morning.

We suspected she surmised what happened and we knew she would never forget her wedding day. Nor would we.

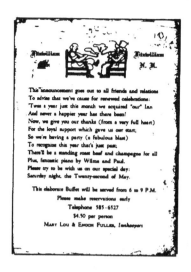

X
'TWAS THE SCHOONER FULLER

Let the Parties Begin

The idea of having special theme parties was the outgrowth of an anniversary dinner dance held to celebrate our first year at the Inn.

That May, I started a tradition that lasted throughout our tenure at the Fitzwilliam Inn. Calling on my creative skills, I wrote poetic invitations and had them printed as postcards.

We had a mailing list of patrons from Hancock and Fitzwilliam plus Red's days at Uxbridge, Tedesco and the Yankee Drummer. Party notices were sent to these people and also former house guests, as we found even those from a distance would make party reservations and book a room for the night.

Each party had a theme based on a seasonal holiday. Some months were "dry" - no holiday - so we would substitute our own form of fiesta based on a current event, particular ethnic theme or Washington, D.C. politicos. Summer was the easiest time to foster a special non-holiday event; the weather was more cooperative for outside activities, particularly if we wanted to involve the swimming pool.

Our creative juices would start flowing as soon as a theme was decided. A special drink would be concocted which, of necessity, required many taste tests, usually taking place late at night; often involving interested house guests or a Mother. "Needs a little more kick to it, Red," became the rallying cry and in would go another half jigger of liquor. Decorations set the stage and created the evening's atmosphere. I made theme costumes for the waitresses, bearing in mind need for mobility as they moved through the dining room. Earle reigned supreme as he came up with innovative recipes and menus that would tie the entire evening together.

At the Uxbridge Inn, Red employed Wilma and Paul Bordeleau to play for dancing in the lounge. They were delighted to be asked to entertain for our parties in Fitzwilliam. Paul played our piano and Wilma played her portable electronic keyboard. Their music was very danceable and Paul's arrangements were popular with our clientele.

The 80 pound Steamboat Round of Beef
with Red, Earle, Mary Lou and Reino Lilback

That first anniversary party was my introduction to a Steamship Round of Beef and a magnificent thing it was; weighing 80 pounds, it was the entire haunch of a steer. Earle needed help getting it in and out of the oven as well as moving it to the buffet table. Once positioned under infrared heat lamps, it was an elegant sight. Reino Lilback, Earle's part time assistant, would do the carving as guests moved along the serving line. Earle shrank from the limelight and even carving his own "beautiful beast" was too much. One other person, such as the baker, also served behind the line and answered questions about the various dishes. Two banquet tables would be set up in front of the swinging doors to the kitchen, providing easy access for refilling platters.

Many customers arrived outfitted according to the party theme. For example, there might be a tableful of Indian headdresses; witches hats and false noses; or tattered outfits suitable for a shipwreck. It all added tremendously to the party spirit.

Since tables were reserved for the entire evening, there was no re-seating. Surprised walk-ins, who had no prior knowledge of the event, would be given the option of joining us if there was space available. Wilma and Paul "struck up their instruments" at 9 p.m. and, once the buffet tables were taken away, the dancing began.

You Are Cordially Invited

We averaged six parties a year; including New Year's Eve. Five are highlighted below. Invitations for eight others appear on succeeding pages.

New Year's Eve

Always a gala evening again featuring a Steamship Round and flaming Cherries Jubilee for dessert. We served complimentary champagne at midnight and toasted our guests who, in turn, raised their glasses to us. In memory of our New Year's eve at Hancock, we always fixed peanut butter sandwiches for our supper. It kept us humble in the face of so much success.

Fitzwilliam Inn   Fitzwilliam N. H.

Santa Claus will soon arrive —
We're stuffed with Christmas Cheer;
And while it's still a part of us
Let's think of the New Year!

We hope our plans will fit with yours,
So we can share this night
Of hopefulness and gaiety,
And end the old year right!

It's a great excuse to have a Ball,
That's filled with special fun;
As we kiss old 1970 goodbye
And welcome '71!

A Gala Evening!

Music for Dancing   Champagne at Midnight

Roast Beef Dinner served from 7:00 to 10:30 P. M.

$8.50 per person

Reservations, please!   585-6527

Your Hosts: The Fuller Family

A Night for Skiers

This was an all-out attempt to boost winter business and establish the Inn as an official "aprés ski" gathering place. In conjunction with the Fitzwilliam Ski Area, we planned consecutive Friday night buffets to be served when the slopes closed at 9 p.m. This first event was a big success, but the weather was not always cooperative for skiing and many such evenings were cancelled. Red's special drink for ski night was a Broken Leg. It consisted of hot apple juice, bourbon and a cinnamon stick; delectable after coming in from the cold but it had a "kick" to it because of the heated liquor.

Strictly a Barnyard Event

As the invitation warned, tables were set without silverware, instead guests were issued large aprons for protection. These completely engulfed the wearer eliciting a chuckle or two. The menu consisted of finger foods to follow the "Tom Jones" example.

To set the mood for the evening, we borrowed chickens to peck around on the north lawn as guests arrived. Everything was going smoothly until the cock in charge of the hen harem flew out of his temporary pen. With wings akimbo, half flying and half running, the bird darted across the lawn, the innkeeper in hot pursuit. The guests, convinced the performance was "staged", stood around laughing, as first the bird and then Red dashed from one tree to another.

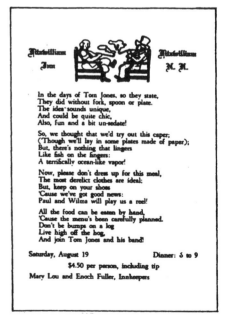

The Cruise of the Schooner Fuller

Summer was a fertile time for party ideas. Polynesian nights and shipwreck parties were both popular and successful. The prize at one such party for best "shipwrecked" attire went to the crew which arrived in a bottomless rowboat, T-shirts on top, bare legs protruding below. "Sunken" door prizes required the winner to dive into the swimming pool to "retrieve" the treasure; usually a bottle of Scotch.

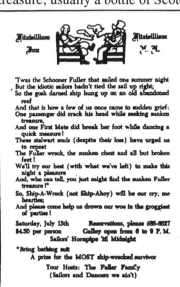

175 and Still Counting

A magnificent birthday cake, adorned with the Inn logo, graced the front hall table for all to see. Everyone signed a scroll which was later framed and hung in honor of the epochal event.

Fitzwilliam Inn **Fitzwilliam N. H.**

October claims Columbus—but, also Hallowe'en;
And there's the biggest puzzle that we have ever seen:

We can't forget old Christopher (courageous and undaunted);
But, overlooking ghosts and such, could have us end up haunted!

We finally decided that we'd combine the two,
As Italian Jack O'Lanterns would really be quite new!

T'will be a special night, all right, and one you won't forget,
As the ghosties and the witches serve up the Spaghett!

So come do homage to old Chris, by whom this world began;
But wear your spookiest of duds and the falsest face you can!

Saturday, October 30	$4.25 per person

Cauldron bubbles from 6 to 9
Witches brew 'til Midnight

Dancing	Prizes for the Best Costumes
Reservations, please!	585-6527

Casa Fullerini

COLUMBUS AND HALLOWE'EN

Fitzwilliam Inn **Fitzwilliam N. H.**

Goodbye, Lyndon! Hello, Who?
We wonder who will follow you?

We've planned a night for LBJ.
Also, Dick and RFK;

And, HHH, Eugene and Rock,
And George and Ronnie, what a flock!

Plus, any others we forgot,
And, surely, there must be a lot.

There's plenty running, that we know:
It's eenie, meenie, minie, mo!

We're having steak and corn and 'taters,
Bread and fruit and red tomaters.

The steak we're pricing by the ounce,
So no one's budget takes a bounce.

The Bordeleaus will play for dancing.
(There won't be many not up prancing.)

If Conventions you can't make this year —
Join us in our own, right here!!

Saturday, June 22	Steaks Broiled: 6 to 9
Reservations, please	Telephone: 585-6527
Mary Lou and Enoch Fuller, Innkeepers	And, Josh!

Dress for the Ranch

GOOD-BYE LYNDON!

Fitzwilliam Inn **Fitzwilliam N. H.**

'Twas Duffy that told Sean McDonald
And O'Hoolihan passed it to Flynn:
That they're wearin' the Green on March 17th
Up at the Fitzwilliam Inn!

Then, O'Hara picked up the story,
Said, "Faith, them Fitzwilliam Colleens
Won't be all that's our color on March 17th:
The drinks will be all shades of green!"

Then Hanrahan said to McMurphy,
"Ha ya heard what they're havin' to eat?"
"Why, ya Irisher bloke, on March 17th
'Tis surely a grand Irish Treat!"

So it's Erin Go Bragh at Fitzwilliam.
Host, McFuller, his Colleens and all
Will be wearin the Green on March 17th
For a good old St. Patrick's Day Ball!

Friday, March 17	Dinner: 6 to 9 p. m.
Reservations, please	Telephone: 585-6527

Door Prize!
Music for Dancing!
$4.25 per person

Yer Hosts: McFuller and the Missus — plus, the wee Lad and Lass!

ERIN GO BRAGH

Fitzwilliam Inn **Fitzwilliam N. H.**

Old Man Fuller had an Inn
Ee - yi ee yi oh!
Where you ain't lived unless you been!
Ee - yi ee yi oh!

He'll have a farm night just for fun
And hopes that everyone will come.

He's serving steak with French Fried 'taters
Bread and corn and red tomaters.

The steak he's pricing by the ounce
So no one's budget takes a bounce.

The Bordeleaus will play for dancing
There won't be many not up prancing.

The livestock will be full of pep
Everyone best watch his step

Yes, Old Man Fuller has an Inn
Ee - yi ee yi oh!
Where you ain't lived unless you been
Ee - yi ee yi oh!

Saturday, June 22	Steaks Broiled: 6 to 9
Reservations, please	Telephone: 585-6527
Mary Lou and Enoch Fuller, Innkeepers	And, Josh!

Dress for the Farm

OLD MACDONALD HAD A FARM

Fitzwilliam Inn — Fitzwilliam N. H.

From the shores, of old Fitzwilliam, by the shining,
    deep pool waters
Comes this message from the Fullers, to the native
    sons and daughters:
Telling Summertime is ended and the glistening
    Fall is coming:
Time for Injun Summer Party; so this call goes out
    a-drumming.
Come to big Fitzwilliam Teepee where the campfire
    will be burning.
Join our tribe, the Manayung Tribe, bring Papoose,
    if you've a yearning;
Feast on corn and beans and turkey; Johnny Cake
    and rice that's wild,
Helpum self from Harvest Basket, do a dance that's
    Injun styled.
Try our brand of firewater
    (Med'cine Man make special tall !)
Heap big noise from Music Makers: friendly Squaw
    and Brave named Paul.
So come and join our Injun Party, havum fun,
    smoke Peace Pipe, too.
Come to Tribal Get-together, whether Apache,
    Creek or Sioux !

Saturday, October 18   Pot Boilum: 6 to 9

Phone: 585-6527 for good Teepee Seat

Pow-wow Leaders: The Fuller Tribe

$3.95 Wampum   Dressum in Best Blanket

INJUN PARTY

Fitzwilliam Inn — Fitzwilliam N. H.

Guten Tag zu der Damen und Herren
From der Fitzelburg Alps we're declaren:
It's "Deutschland über alles";
So come zu der Palast
Where das Lederhosen we're wearen.

We'll be haben der Wiener und Schnitzel
(Gemacht by der Koch named Earl "Kitzel".)
Mit Knuckle von Schwein
Und Beer von der Stein
Zu please every Frau and her Fritzel!

There'll be Muzic by Wilma and Paul
Und der singen will ring through der hall;
There'll be Waltzes von Strauss
So biter come ous
Und we'll say "Danke Schöne" to you all!

Ausverkauf: $3.75 per person   Reservations, please!

Das Alpine Kleid

Mary Lou und Enoch Fuller, die Gasthof Leute   585-6527

Saturday, December 4th   6-9 P.M.

GERMAN NIGHT

Fitzwilliam Inn — Fitzwilliam N. H.

Bonjour Madmoiselle. Madame et Monsieur
Pour le finest of evenings centimes can procure
We offer our "Nuit de Fitzwilliam" à vous
And here's what we're planning (but just entre nous):
We're bringing Paree to Fitzwilliam's old shores
Complete avec fashions which each girl adores.
We'll start with escargots (those cute curly snails)
And move to Suzettes served in flaming crêpe veils!
There will also be featured some cold Vichysoisse
Plus other carte items: pomme de terre et green pois.
Le Vin de la Jour to spark up the night
And "Adagio Dancers" make the bistro just right
Wilma and Paul provide le Whoopiree
Et le grande final est: les "Cheris" Jubilee!
La piece de resistance we shall not disclose
But you can be sure 'twill be à vôtre chose;
So take up la plume without further ado
Mark August 27th et. Merci Beaucoup!

Dress a la Left Bank

$5.00 per person   Please Make Reservations Very Early

Les delectables servant 6 to 9 P.M.

Mary Lou and Enoch Fuller   Telephone: 585 - 6527

PARISIAN NIGHT

Fitzwilliam Inn — Fitzwilliam N. H.

There once was a man we call Saint
Who started a custom real quaint:
Saying "life is a bore",
He went to the store
And bought paper and lots of red paint!

Then he made up a bunch of love rhymes
Wrote them out on red, heart-shaped signs;
Mailed them off to the girls
With the prettiest curls;
And from that was born St. Valentines!

So let's honor this blessed old gent,
By whom love notes were really first sent.
We'll hang hearts on the wall
Throw a Valentine Ball
And hope here is where you'll say you went!

$4.00 per person   Lovers' Delectables 6 to 9

Love Songs and Love Potion served up until Midnight

Mary Lou and Enoch Fuller, Keepers of the Love Nest

Saturday, February 11

Telephone: 585 - 6527

ST. VALENTINE'S

And the Parties Went On

Our party nights were always successful and a great deal of fun for us. Plus, it was gratifying to realize how many people derived pleasure from our efforts. "Party fever" was catching and, as word spread, customers clamored for more; there was nowhere else in the Monadnock region one could go for an evening of dinner and dancing, enhanced by the colorful antics of a staid and conservative New England innkeeper and his staff. For many magical evenings, the old but venerable Fitzwilliam Inn, also had an opportunity to "have a ball".

A Party Night

XI
ONE CAR, TWO DRIVERS

Dealing with Leftovers

During our first years at the Inn, the guest rooms were filled very sporadically; especially winter and spring. This situation prompted another of Red's maxims, "There is nothing more perishable than a room that goes empty overnight: you can't get any of your money back by 'heating it up and serving it as a leftover' the next day!"

One local wag advised, "This place won't make a profit unless you turn it into a 'hot-bed hostelry'." This so offended Red's training and sensibilities, he began to dread seeing the wagster coming. To further rub salt into the wound, the fellow would quote from the latest stock market averages on a new chain known as Best Western Motels. This, the erstwhile "advisor" bragged, was stock he owned.

In winter, if ski reports were favorable, guest rooms were filled on weekends. Families came to Fitzwilliam on a variety of missions: to utilize Al Bicknell's local ski area, or use the Inn as "home base" as they journeyed to more challenging slopes farther north.

Summer tourists came out of the cities seeking the nurturing balm of our stone walls and white wooden churches. These were often a restless sort, usually dissatisfied with our lack of amenities, such as elevators, TV's and telephones. Red would counter with "If you're looking for a plastic motel, it's best you move on." And often the retort would be, "I had no idea the place was so primitive: there aren't even room keys."

Others, who adjusted easily to only being able to lock their rooms from the inside, would stay but invariably asked, "Is it always so quiet here?"

For better or worse, Red concluded we needed a couple of house guests who would, *if things worked out,* stay at the Inn for an extended period of time. He pointed out, "room revenue from this type of arrangement will underwrite some of our on-going costs."

Red made his intentions known through connections in the industry. He especially approached his fellow members in an exclusive New York club, whose basic membership requirements were being a Shriner, as well as a hotelier. By spring of our second year our first such guest had arrived.

Madame René de Pardeau

Close to 80, hair the color of orange Kool-Aid, lips and cheeks a bright "tangee", René de Pardeau descended upon us.

We had dispatched Bob Berry to the train in Springfield, Massachusetts to collect her and, when asked about the return trip with his passenger, he was barely able to communicate. His amateur attempt at sarcasm was obvious: *"You'll* find out. I found out, now *you're* gonna find out."

Indeed, we started to "find out" the very next morning when Randy, the college student helping Abbie with housekeeping, came hurrying downstairs wanting to know if we had a spare douche bag. *"Douche bag,* Randy?" I asked, certain that I had misunderstood the blushing young man. "Yes, Madame de Pardeau says she left hers in New York and needs one immediately so she can finish her 'twa-letty'." As we had no lend-lease douche bags, I sent him back to assure her I would get her specifics and pick one up in Keene. Red would be undone if, for want of a douche bag, we lost our first long-termer.

When Madame finally appeared downstairs, she was clad in a "sports outfit". Starting with a hair ribbon and moving on down to a knit sweater with built-in bosom, shorts that revealed all 80 years of her legs and ending in bobby socks and wedgies, circa 1942. We labeled this her "cruising" attire because she would spend time after breakfast in a seductive stroll through the public rooms.

About 11 a.m. she would return to her room and switch from shorts to pedal pushers for lunch. This was her time to station herself at the first table in the dining room. From here she commanded a view of all who entered or left and could monitor nearby conversations. She had no qualms about joining in on subjects that piqued her interest, often becoming argumentative if the gist of the discussion was not to her liking. There was no topic on which she did not claim to be expert.

Her overtures to a group of Troy Mills executives was her downfall. When the men complained vociferously to Red that they did not appreciate her advances and suggestive body language, he was forced to speak to her and she responded, "I don't need scolding from you."

In the evening she often dressed formally, and always so on weekends. She made the front parlour her private salon. Here she would sit like a red-headed spider waiting to throw a net over an unsuspecting victim. Once a suitable prey had been spotted, her flirtatious behaviour would begin. One guest confided that she had even slipped him a note with her room number on it.

After a month of this, all attempts by Red and me to rein in her search for a male conquest had failed. The Mothers met with equal frustration when their efforts to include her in a jigsaw puzzle or a game of Canasta were declined. "All she can talk about are the men she's known or wants to find," Mimi expostulated. Abbie was almost rendered speechless; never having seen anything to compare with her. "At her age, she should be ashamed of herself," was her reaction.

Under pressure plus a few suggestions that the Inn was not living up to her expectations, Madame de Pardeau finally checked out, giving as an excuse that she preferred the heat in New York City to our dull town. Abbie helped her pack, making sure that her New Hampshire douche bag made it into her luggage.

Mrs. Langford Eidelmeyer

Mrs. Eidelmeyer's secretary wrote us expressing interest in a two-month stay for her employer. The letter continued, "Langford Eidelmeyer's literary achievements had entitled him, and thence his widow, to time at the MacDowell Colony, but her eligibility is long past. We're looking for a worthy substitute." The Eidelmeyers had friends in the area who had stayed at the Inn and found it "charming"; unquestionably it met all their criteria.

Red had me respond in the affirmative regarding space availability. An answer arrived promptly and we selected Room 12, on the south side of the Inn, as a good choice. Recently vacated by Madame de Pardeau, it had a double bed and private bath. The view from the window was of Richmond Road and afforded a glimpse of the town hall steeple and the common as well; a perfect room for a single occupant.

A week prior to Mrs. Eidelmeyer's arrival, we received a postal notice that a box of perishables was being held at the post office. As soon as we saw it we should have had the good sense to prevent Mrs. Eidelmeyer's arrival at all costs. The box, 18 inches square, was lavishly labeled, *"Medicines: Refrigerate Immediately"*. Too late to reverse things, Mrs. Eidelmeyer arrived at Keene's Dillant-Hopkins Airport. Bob Berry ferried her to the Inn.

She was a diminutive person, almost fragile; but despite her frail appearance she had an iron determination and set about to bend us all to her will the moment she set foot in the door.

"I must have some sustenance immediately," she cried. "My heart is pounding; fetch two pills from the blue bottle in my purse."

I led her carefully into the dining room and, at her direction, "fetched" tea and a "simple bread and butter sandwich".

Once fortified she began the climb to the second floor. It must have taken 15 minutes as she came to a full stop after each riser. I followed along behind. Abbie went on ahead with Bob to deposit the luggage. Red stood in the hallway watching our slow ascent. I threw him a withering look and mouthed, "You've done it again!"

From the first day Mrs. Eidelmeyer was in residence, she required more service than we had to offer. It began with the re-arrangement of the room because the head of the bed was on an outside wall. On the verge of tears, she said "I simply can't tolerate it!" We doled out her medication five times a day from *the box* now lodged in Earle's walk-in. Room service was required for meals when she was unable to "go over the stairs". Abbie was always on tap to handle the myriad of other orders that emanated from Room 12.

It was too much. We were not staffed for such a demanding guest. "She needs a nurse-companion," Abbie told Red. And so, after only a two-week stay, a friend of Mrs. Eidelmeyer's in Jaffrey Center was persuaded to collect her.

Cornelia Davenport

Edmund Davenport contacted us by telephone from New York City to inquire about residence for his Aunt Cornelia. "She has no close family except her dog, Toby; just needs a home. There's plenty of money to pay for whatever you have available. My sister had her for two years, but she's to be married and Cornelia can't stay there. She's over 80, but no trouble. Please say you'll take her."

To everyone's shock and dismay, Red agreed to take in Cornelia and, in due course, she arrived with her nephew, who had driven her up from New York. Toby, in his carrier, was carted upstairs and, along with Cornelia's old fashioned carpet bags and assorted paper sacks, was deposited in Room 11. After Mrs. Eidelmeyer and the Madame, we had concluded there was a jinx on Room 12.

Cornelia had white, naturally wavy hair, worn in a short bob; her dark eyes were snappy and alert. Although Edmund had told us her age, her agility and youthful attributes belied it. She had no problem leashing up Toby to make many trips down the stairs, out the front door and down the steep granite steps. We discovered that Toby, attracted by the permanent mud over our septic system, used the ferns we had planted to hide that eyesore. Over the time Cornelia was with us, Toby succeeded in rendering that area completely bald.

One day she asked about using the swimming pool. I was certain the question was purely rhetorical: at her age she surely was not considering a swim. How naive I was! Cornelia descended the back stairs from her room and stepped out onto a Patio filled with people.

In a vintage 1915 bathing suit, with sleeved tunic over knee-length trunks and white rubber bathing shoes, she threaded her way through the tables to the delight of everyone.

Summoned by a waitress, I hurried to the Patio just in time to watch Cornelia plunge into the pool. "The water never gets above 65 degrees - she'll perish," I thought. But she was tougher than that and made two round trips of the pool before climbing out. The Patio crowd cheered and clapped.

During the Christmas season she had me purchase paper, envelopes and a set of watercolor paints with which she produced packets of impression-istic greeting cards. Abbie described the clothes line strung up in her room where masses of cards were hang up to dry. Inn guests snapped them up from Fulla Gifts and we gave Cornelia a 60-40 split on all sales. Soon mail orders began to come in as guests returned home and showed off her work.

Cornelia never missed a meal in the dining room and attended all our party nights clad in her turn-of-the-century dresses. We loved her gentle-ness and soft-spoken ways. She was no trouble.

Cornelia Davenport at the buffet table

Then either senility, or per-haps Alzheimer's disease, be-gan to manifest itself. Subtle at first, the mental changes in Cornelia became more dra-matic with time. She com-plained to Red that "the house-keeper is giving me wet tow-els every morning and she's putting poison in the closet for Toby." Abbie, who was al-ways so willing to help, took the brunt of her anger and ac-cusations.

She heard voices coming from her closet and was sure everyone was persecuting her. When she refused to bathe and change her clothes it was clear we were not equipped to handle another long-termer.

We hated to think that Cornelia would be institution-alized and separated from Toby; but the Inn could not be that institution. Edmund made arrangements to have Cornelia picked up at the Inn and the last we saw of her she was climbing into a taxi. Toby, on his leash, jumped in beside her.

One Car, Two Drivers

We had other guests who stayed for considerable periods of time, some because they were retiring to Fitzwilliam and building a house. One couple was Evelyn and Harry Inkster, who had been such a comfort to the Daley family during the tragedy at the wedding reception. Often we were the first personal contact for potential residents and felt privileged to extoll the virtues of the town. In some cases our wholehearted devotion to the Monadnock region was the deciding factor in favor of Fitzwilliam.

At the time, we were unaware what a red-letter day it was when we received the reservation from a travel agent, requesting a twin-bed room for a Dr. and Mrs. Hugo Paganelli for a two-week stay. A great piece of business we thought at first, then quickly tempered that idea as we studied their complicated name and read the additional reservation stipulation: "To be met at Brattleboro train station by *one car and two drivers.*"

With a sneer of contempt I said to Red, "More weirdos!" The number of drivers required *was* a mystery but Red, accompanied by Bob Berry, drove off to meet the train not knowing what to expect.

When they returned with the two guests, Red was in high humor. His enthusiasm for the Paganellis was contagious. He explained Hugo had rented a car from a Brattleboro agency but, because he did not keep a car in the city his driving skills were rusty: he needed the second person to drive the rental car to Fitzwilliam.

"We only wanted a car so we could go around Laurel Lake," Naomi Paganelli explained. "We have a lot of memories from there. My sister and I attended Fleur de Lis, while my folks stayed at Gates Cottage. Then, years later, Hugo and I honeymooned at the lake. We walked up to a local hot dog stand every day for lunch." The Paganellis were wonderful guests: participative, conversational and interested in us. We became good friends and looked forward to their return visits.

Putting One and Two Together

The Fitzwilliam Inn had more than twice the number of guest rooms as Hancock and, at first, it took me awhile to mentally match the configuration of the rooms upstairs to the room chart as I stood at the front desk.

Rooms 6, 7 and 8 presented a particularly peculiar problem. They *could* be rented as a three-room suite, with private bath. Originally it was the family quarters of the Blairs, Fitzwilliam innkeepers for forty years in the early 1900's. It was a perfect arrangement for a family, but otherwise it was a "disaster-in-waiting" and could become a hopeless maze of rooms for a desk clerk not alert to the pitfalls. Through the bath attached to Room 6 was Room 7 and, through that, Room 8; *both singles.* Rooms 6 and 8 each accessed a main hallway and could be rented independently. If that was the case, Room 7 *could not* be sold. I had learned that the hard way when I checked complete strangers into each of the three, virtually trapping the

Room 7 occupant. Since all our rooms were filled that night, everyone was forced to make the best of a difficult situation.

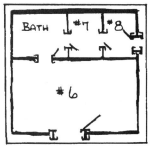

Charles and Madge Sweeney had been guests at the Inn during the Bicknell days and preferred Room 6. On their first visit after our arrival as innkeepers, I was determined to be gracious and welcoming. So intent, in fact, that I neglected to enter the Sweeney's arrival in Room 6 on the front desk chart.

Henry Fish, a dye salesman to Noone Mills in Peterborough, also liked Room 6. He arrived when Red was on duty at the front desk, and was checked into the *same* room where I had lodged the Sweeneys.

Henry Fish, going up to his room, must have passed Charles Sweeney going down the stairs and out to his car. The timing could not have been more precise: at the exact moment Henry Fish opened the door to Room 6, Madge Sweeney stepped out of the bathroom. Except for the towel around her hair, *she was completely nude!*

Henry Fish backed hastily from the room and, his face the picture of an impending explosion, presented himself once again at the front desk.

No one, except Madge Sweeney, was more shocked than I when my error was discovered. She refused to come down for dinner saying, "I don't ever want to see that man again!" Her husband, who had missed the mortifying encounter entirely, was struck by the comedy of it all and threw back his head and laughed loud and long.

It was not until Henry Fish had checked out after breakfast the next morning that Madge Sweeney ventured downstairs.

The Buzzer Takes a Holiday

Dick Rogers had a room reservation but by midnight, when he had not arrived, Red came up to our apartment. He expressed his annoyance at the thought we would be wakened by the buzzer "at some un-Godly hour" when Rogers finally showed up. In the morning we compared notes and, because neither of us had heard the buzzer, concluded we had been "stiffed" by a no-show.

During breakfast, a single man about 40, appeared in the dining room. When he was seated, he said to me, "By the way, I'm Dick Rogers. My car broke down last night so I arrived very late. I rang the front doorbell, but got no answer."

I assumed Mimi had heard him at the door and let him in, but Rogers went on, "I walked around the building trying all the doors and finally saw the fire escape. Because the snow had piled up enough on the bulkhead, I was able to jump for the end of the ladder, pull it down and climb up to a second-floor window." This turned out to be Room 12 which I knew had been occupied. Dick Rogers continued his incredible story, "The window was easy to open and I crawled in. When the people in bed didn't stir, I let myself out into the hall and took number 14 across the way." .

Nothing in our ten years at the Inn ever compared to this bit of creative problem-solving!

Teeth on the Edge

It was New Year's Day. The front parlour was crowded with noisy house guests eager to continue the celebration begun the evening before. The Eggnog Party that brought them together had become a tradition from the first year we owned the Inn. It preceded a lavish New England buffet breakfast featuring the usual eggs, sausage, creamed chipped beef and homemade biscuits, along with baked beans and hot apple pie with cheese.

I officiated over a bowl of eggnog laced with brandy, all the while fighting a fatigue hangover from hostessing the dinner dance until the wee hours. Suddenly a little girl pushed her way through the throng of adults; tears ran down her cheeks. "Grandma said to find Mary Lou and give her this note," she sobbed. "She says we'll have to leave if you can't help her, and I want to ski today."

I unfolded the scrap of paper and discovered the reason for her grandmother's distress. She had written, "Have you found a set of upper teeth? I left mine in the dining room last night. Please locate them and Shelly can bring them up to me." The note was signed, "Claire Sheridan".

Excusing myself, I grabbed Shelly's hand and we ran up the steps to the second floor. I rapped on the door of Room 5. Mrs. Sheridan opened it immediately. Her toothless mouth was drawn into a bow to keep her lips from disappearing.

Suppressing an urge to laugh, I questioned Mrs. Sheridan about her table assignment and the circumstances that led up to the loss of her dentures. In the absence of teeth, her tongue had free reign in her mouth impairing her diction and lending an even more comedic note to the already amusing situation. She explained, "Food got caught, making them hurt; so I took the teeth out and laid them on the edge of my plate. I can't believe I didn't notice they weren't in my mouth when I left the dining room. Shelly wants to ski today but I can't stay in this condition."

Assuring Mrs. Sheridan I would do my best, I returned to the parlour, filled any empty eggnog cups and headed for the kitchen. I was quite sure I already knew where Mrs. Sheridan's dentures had spent the night and shuddered at what lay ahead.

I asked Abbie to help and, bundled in our coats, we went out the back kitchen door. With Wendell supporting the full garbage pail over the edge of an empty bucket, Abbie and I slowly pulled the garbage from one to the other using longhandled wooden spoons.

Incredibly, the dentures surfaced midway through the search. After running them under the hottest water at the dish sink, Abbie wrapped them in a napkin and delivered them to Mrs. Sheridan.

A Phony Firecracker

It was the 4th of July, always a quiet holiday around the Inn; Red and I were just returning from a few hours at the pool. As we walked out of the bathhouse gate and down to our apartment entrance off the parking lot, there was a loud pop. "Early firecracker," Red observed.

We were changing our clothes when there was an urgent banging at the door of our living quarters.

When Red answered the knock Harry Mason stood in the doorway. "You better come quickly. I came back from Keene and found my wife on the floor of our room. She shot herself; she's dead." Shirtless, Red hurried after Harry, shouting at me to call the rescue squad.

Alice Mason *was* dead. She had shot herself in the temple with a small-caliber handgun. "No mess at all," Red reported. "But because of the way she died, we have to have the sheriff and the coroner come to talk with Harry and me."

Bizarre as this experience was for us and the Mothers, who had spoken to Alice Mason just hours before, more was to come.

Services for Alice were held at a mortuary in Winchendon, Massachusetts. Afterwards, Harry moved in with friends who lived across town.

He continued to come into the dining room periodically and eventually started dating one of our waitresses. In six months they were married and literally "drove off into the sunset". I sensed that Harry had gone without so much as a backward glance, or thought, of poor Alice.

How intuitive my feeling proved to be: four years after Harry and his new wife left Fitzwilliam I had a phone call from the funeral home in Winchendon. "Did I know where Mr. Mason could be reached?" they inquired. I replied in the negative. Expressing the smooth solicitude that only such folks can muster, he said, "Too bad. Mr. Mason told us he'd be in for his wife's ashes, but he never came back.

A guest's self-portrait
sent as a postcard to the innkeeper
in appreciation for a memorable stay at the Fitzwilliam Inn

Fulla Gift Shop

XII
HOUSE OF THIEVES

First Came Pride

My wholehearted enjoyment of interacting with our guests was jarred off-center early in our Fitzwilliam days. Red, who was neither a student of human behaviour nor a connoisseur of aesthetics, was more stunned and outraged than I over the foul play that began to invade our serene environment. For me, the hardest to absorb was the disturbing sense of having misplaced my trust in people. Because I was forthright: a "what you see, is what you get" kind of person, I in turn accepted others at face value.

Red and I, and especially the Mothers, took considerable pride in the unique touches that added so much to the Inn's atmosphere and Early American decor. Sadly, I was to discover there lurked a darkness that endangered these very things we cherished and enjoyed having around us.

Next to the telephone stand in the upstairs hallway was a small antique chair with wooden seat. Here and there, along the hallways, were others that were similar. At auctions or garage sales, I had picked up enough hand-braided seat covers so each chair was adorned. Made of bright colors, old and mended, they added a touch of the period and brightened the halls.

Bottle collecting was at its peak in the 60's and I learned about "picking" in old foundations and "home dumps" from friends who dealt commercially in these treasures. I was fortunate to have found a half-dozen old medicine bottles whose original glass had darkened to a soft lavender. Displayed in the dining room adjacent to the four window tables, they complemented the dishes and plates on the little shelves and Mimi's array of African violets on the windowsill.

Red had inherited a quantity of pewter dating back to the 1800's. It consisted of a large serving platter, ten plates (six large and four small), a coffee pot and a tea service. We had a shelf put up on the north wall of the dining room on which I arranged the pewter. The dining room glowed with the attention it received.

Naive to a fault and impressed with my own creativity, I never tired of looking at these additions. But before long, my self-serving attitude jinxed their longevity.

One weekend in summer, when the guest rooms were filled with antique dealers who had "set up" at the town hall in preparation for the next day's antiques show, three of the small pewter plates disappeared. I was speechless when the loss was discovered. Red demonstrated how easy it would be to slip the small plates into a jacket pocket or tote bag. I was heart broken all the same and removed the remaining pewter, replacing it with less desirable tin pieces.

It was not long before the majority of my precious seat covers found their way into homeward-bound suitcases.

The bottles were next; slower to go, but go they did. It was terribly disappointing to realize the thieves were probably the very house guests with whom I had had warm conversations while, behind my back, they congratulated themselves over my naiveté.

Mysterious Disappearance

It was a Sunday night in winter. As was our custom on Sundays, we had closed the dining room at 8 p.m. and the Pub at 10. Although there were still a few lingering guests in the Pub, Dick, our part-time bartender, had issued "last call" and the Inn doors were already locked. As Red would recount many times afterward, "There were only seven of us: myself, Dick the bartender, two Franklin Pierce College instructors and three house painters who were staying with us while they worked on a place on the Old Jaffrey Road. I knew I'd have to let the college guys out, but I'd locked the doors because it was after 10 and I didn't want anyone walking in."

While the customers finished their drinks, Red went to the cash register across from the Pub doorway and balanced-out the day's receipts. He ran a tape of the Pub and dining room slips and counted the cash and checks. As was his habit, he bundled everything together in a rubber band and set it on the counter next to the register.

When the Franklin Pierce instructors got up to leave, Red walked to the side door with them, said "Good-night" and let them out. He re-locked the door and returned to the Pub. The painters went up to their third floor room.

Dick was bustling around clearing tables and washing glasses, apparently hurrying to go home. Red reached for his day's receipts to add the last bar slips and accompanying cash. It was then he discovered his packet of receipts and money was not where he had put it.

I had gone upstairs as soon as the dining

Red at hallway cash register
(scene of the mysterious disappearance)

room closed and had retired when Red burst into the room. "Please tell me you came down and picked up the day's receipts." "No," I answered, "I went to bed right off. I've been here all along." "Well, the money's been stolen," he cried. "I'm going to call Webb and get him over here. There were only seven of us in the Pub; the doors were locked! I knew I hadn't taken it; that's why I thought you might have come down. I trust Dick and the Franklin Pierce fellas were with me at the door. It has to be those house painters."

I jumped out of bed, threw on some clothes and hurried after him down through the Inn. Red was already on the phone: "Webb, I don't care that you haven't finished the police course; put on your uniform and come over. Please!"

Webb Sherman, once Fitzwilliam's Town Clerk, had only recently become our chief of police. This was the result of a town meeting showdown between the previous chief and the townspeople over the need to hire an additional deputy. The vote went against the chief and he walked off the job right then and there. Webb, who knew nothing about police work, agreed to take the position, but freely admitted he needed formal instruction. He was in the process of acquiring this by attending classes in Concord.

When he finally arrived at the Inn this particular Sunday evening, he was attired in his full uniform with all the badges; a gun holstered on his hip. Even with all his regalia, it was hard to distinguish him from Barney Fife, Andy Griffith's deputy on the _Mayberry_ TV show.

Convinced the thieves were under his roof in Room 27, Red went upstairs and asked the painters to return to the Pub.

Webb, doing his best to look the part, swaggered in and sat opposite the three men. To my amazement, the first words out of his mouth in a shaking voice were, "I'll have a beer, Enoch." Perhaps realizing that was not the primary thing to consider, he paused to mend his voice in an attempt to bring some authority into play. Instead, he further compounded the situation by addressing the painters with, "I'm still in training as the new chief so I'm not certain what the procedure is here or whether I have any legal right to question you, but I'd appreciate your cooperation."

Red beckoned Dick and me out into the hall and said, "While Webb's got these men down here, you two go up and search their room." I ducked into the dining room and grabbed the fireplace poker for some sort of security and we set off upstairs. The room was easy to search; there were just three satchels laid out on the beds. Dick was all for going through the bags, but I felt we had no right even to be in the room so, after a perfunctory look around, we hurried back downstairs before we could get trapped by the painters' return.

Red was sure the money had been taken while he was letting the Franklin Pierce men out the door and he kept pushing Webb's questioning accordingly, "Which of you went to the men's room when I stepped away from the register?" he kept persisting. "None of us did," they replied. "We were sitting here in the Pub all the time until we went upstairs."

Webb turned his attention to Dick and, prefacing the interrogation with the same disclaimer concerning his lack of knowledge about police work, he asked what Dick had seen and heard; had he been in the Pub and able to observe the painters' movements. Dick re-stated everything he had previously told Red and me.

As time wore on it became painfully clear that Webb was getting nowhere with his uncertain approach in uncovering the thief. At no time did he suggest a body-search but, finally at Red's urging, agreed to call the Cheshire County Sheriff's Office to get permission. After a lengthy phone conversation, Webb returned to the Pub and asked the painters to empty their pockets onto the table. When this was done he "patted down" each of them and, having discovered nothing, allowed them to return to their room.

Dick offered to empty *his* pockets and, even before receiving a reply,

took everything out and then raised his arms for Webb to "pat" him too.

Webb made out his official report covering the loss. He gave Red a copy and headed for home with the parting remark, "Sorry I couldn't do any better for you, Enoch."

No one was sorrier than Red. His face was flushed and he was popping sugar cubes into his mouth to prevent an insulin reaction.

Dick went home and the two of us sat in the Pub while Red once again went through the list of suspects. I finally persuaded him to go upstairs to bed.

The next morning he was on the phone to our insurance agent, Henry Scarsdale, in Troy. He went through the entire story ending with, "Henry, please get the necessary claim forms to me as soon as possible. We're only talking about $600, but at this slow time of year I need every penny".

Later in the day Henry Scarsdale called back. I was standing next to Red when he took the call. "*Not* covered?" he barked. "Not *covered! Not covered?* Why *isn't* it covered? The money's *gone."* Henry explained, "There's no proof that the cash was stolen, Enoch; nor did you lose it in a fire. It's considered a 'mysterious disappearance', and you're not insured for that."

"*Not insured?* What kind of a half-assed agent are you to sell me a worthless piece of paper?" he bellowed. The telephone was unnecessary: Henry could have heard him all the way to Troy without it.

The loss affected us terribly. But we recovered from the blow and eventually were able to share a laugh over the story of Webb in his uniform, beer in hand, apologizing to potential criminals for his lack of police skills.

In the spring, when the snows had melted, the packet of receipts was discovered on the ground outside the men's room window. It suddenly struck us that it could easily have been Dick who had purloined Red's money. He must been the one to go into the men's room, pocket the cash and carefully drop the worthless slips out the window where he knew they would be hidden in the crevice by the corner of the building.

Thinking back to Dick's over-eager attitude when we were in the painters' room the night of the theft, and his desire to be searched along with the other suspects, this seemed a likely possibility. Although he began to ingratiate himself by offering to take the Mothers on afternoon excursions, it was difficult to consider him a thief: he was a decent young fellow. Coincidently, shortly after the discovery of the slips, he announced he was moving to Florida. We never saw him again, but the sting of the mysterious disappearance lingered on.

"I Need Your Money"

Red decided the Inn needed a night watchman. He had considered it for some time but the "mysterious disappearance" and our constant concern about fire was the final catalyst that motivated him to take action. After Dick Roger's escapade up the fire escape because no one answered the door bell, he also realized we should have a night desk clerk.

Arthur Vaine, a retired security guard, fit the bill. Red trained him in the duties which included an hourly patrol of the second and third floor halls and periodic checks of the kitchen and back door areas. He made the front desk his headquarters where he could answer the telephone and help anyone who came to the Inn door.

It was almost midnight on a Saturday night. The Inn was officially closed;

everyone had either left or retired to their rooms, including me and the Mothers. The side door was still unlocked because Red was expecting some arrivals momentarily. He was reviewing that reservation with Arthur, preparing to turn over the "helm" to him.

Red still needed to balance-out but, just as he was about to leave Arthur, the Inn door banged open and a tall, thin figure entered wearing a bandana over his face; showing just his eyes.

Thinking the intruder was a local prankster bent on playing a practical joke on the innkeeper, Red made a grab for the "mask" saying, "What kind of trick do you think you're playing?"

Suddenly a new complexion was put on everything when the man pulled a gun from his jacket pocket. The weapon shook in his hand as he pointed it at Red and said, "I need your money; open the register."

On top of the front desk sat the antique cash register used to ring up the gift shop sales. Made of oak, it was large, imposing and could clearly hold a large amount of bills and coin.

Also at the end of the desk, hung Red's ATO fraternity paddle from his university days. He kept it there for no other reason than to attract the attention of any "brothers" who might stop at the Inn.

On this particular night, the paddle became potentially deadly in the hand of Arthur Vaine as he snatched it from its hook and raised it on high, intending to bring it crashing down on the brigand. But he was caught in the act as the robber turned in time to avoid the blow. "Drop it!" he commanded. Arthur did as he was told. This action only served to excite the man and, pushing his way behind the front desk, he yanked the telephone wires from the wall. Then, gesturing with the gun, he waved Red over to the register and repeated, "Open it!"

Not wanting to reveal the existence of the main register around the corner, Red attempted to throw the burglar off by saying, "I've already been to the night depository: there's no money in here."

"I said, open it. I'll decide if there's anything in it." Red opened the drawer, dreading even the loss of Mimi's small sales, but all that greeted them was her neat pile of wrapped pennies totalling $7.00.

The bandit grabbed the penny rolls and bolted for the door shouting over his shoulder, "I'll be back!" After a few minutes, Red and Arthur locked the door and tried to identify the getaway car through the window. But it was too dark and the robber had been too quick. Nevertheless, Webb was notified but never gave chase. Instead he came to the Inn the next morning to take down Red's statement. Webb's theory was the hold-up was caused by too many bad bets at the Hinsdale Trotting Park. The man was probably desperate to recoup his losses and, when he saw the Inn lights on, decided he had nothing more to lose.

"That's a good one, Enoch: $7.00 in pennies; wonder he didn't shoot you in disgust!"

107

New Wallpaper and Paint - Front of 2nd Floor Hall

Parlour showing the Fringed Curtains

THE KEY
The Innkeeper's Symbol

XIII
POLITICS AND PATRIOTISM

Viet Nam

Red was vehement when it came to defending his position on certain subjects, particularly politics and patriotism. During the 1960's, the war in Viet Nam was an issue that evoked the best and worst from the innkeeper. Once having taken a stand, he would either brow-beat the opposition into agreement, or they walked away tossing back an unflattering remark.

As our time in Fitzwilliam lengthened, the more Red used the Pub as his "bully pulpit". Here he had a captive audience and seldom hesitated to get involved in discussions centering on the Viet Nam conflict; often delivering a scathing sermon.

The war, its attendant riots and demonstrations, the burning of draft cards and the blasphemy toward the flag were all events that provoked an instantaneous reaction.

Also, it was widely reported

Red behind the Pub bar

in the local and national press that colleges and universities were lowering their admission standards, allegedly in return for large donations from families bent on protecting sons from the draft.

The stage was set for a confrontation one Saturday night as Red and I relaxed in the Pub after the dining room closed. At a nearby table sat parents whose son had been reported missing in Viet Nam.

Red was commiserating with the couple and going on heatedly about "draft dodgers" hiding out in institutes of higher learning, making disparaging remarks about a school where, he said, "Things like that happen all the time. How do you think they're getting a new library and new dorms?"

Our bartender that night was a college student. With the increased business we were doing, Red had taken him on for part-time work. His name was Wally and in response to Red's diatribe about new college buildings, he said, "Not everyone feels the same as you about Viet Nam or the need for the U.S. to be involved. It's my right as an American to object."

Red glared at the boy, trying to shut him up with a scorching look. But Wally kept on, pointing out, "The National Guard had no right to fire on those Kent State students either."

In the presence of the family with an MIA son, it got too much for Red. He jumped to his feet and marched over to the bar saying, "It's a darn good thing your father has money to keep you out of the draft, you're too much of a coward to fight!"

A look of complete hatred came over Wally's face and he smashed his fist into the innkeeper's nose. Blood cascaded down Red's shirtfront and I rushed for a bar towel to staunch the flow. Holding the towel to his face, Red ordered Wally out of the Inn.

This should have been a lesson, but Red was highly principled and continued using his "bully pulpit" whenever he felt the cause warranted.

Good-bye, Dick

Red was most passionate about politics: it was his favorite topic. If innkeeping was a vocation, then politics was his avocation. It was a birthright of a New Hampshire native to be a conservative Republican. Through all his growing-up years, politics was constantly in the forefront due to Enoch, Sr.'s long career in the state house. But any direct participation in the active political arena was not for Red: his diabetes was a drain on his energy; he simply did not have the stamina, or personality, for campaigning.

Red used the Inn as a Republican bastion and offered it to all manner of New Hampshire office-seekers including Governor Mel Thomson and Senator Jim Cleveland. This spread to encompass presidential hopefuls George Romney and Barry Goldwater, both of whom came through Fitzwilliam on campaign swings.

Richard Nixon's 1968 run for the presidency against Democrat Hubert

Humphrey lit a bonfire of enthusiasm in Red. After all, he was still smarting over Nixon's loss to Kennedy in 1960! He contacted the Republican state chairman and asked to be assigned a task that would help further the campaign in the Monadnock region. He was offered the post of Richmond-Troy-Fitzwilliam coordinator. As a result the Mothers and I were faced with boxes of envelopes to address, into which Red tirelessly stuffed Nixon "news".

When it was announced that Nixon was going to speak at the Keene Junior High School, it sparked such a frenzy in Red he could think of little else as the day approached.

Nixon's travel plans were publicized a week ahead of his arrival: his campaign plane would land at Dillant-Hopkins Airport and Dick and his wife, Pat, would be driven to the junior high.

Red was in a fever of anticipation as we sat in the auditorium waiting for the candidate to appear. He squirmed like a ten-year old at a Saturday matinee: looking this way and that, waving to acquaintances and finally spinning around in his seat to keep an eye on the back of the auditorium.

We had arrived early and were seated near the front; Red had an aisle seat. Finally the Nixons appeared and began to make their way to the stage. Red murmured more to himself than to me, "There's just something about him." I thought he was in danger of swooning as his hero drew closer. In "the presence" at last, he had the temerity to reach out and touch Nixon as he passed.

I had brought my camera hoping to snap a picture of the Nixons during the evening. Red had other ideas: when the applause ended and the audience started to leave, he grabbed my hand saying, "Get the camera ready." We dashed onto the stage; Red rushed over to Nixon and seized his hand. The candidate was momentarily immobilized in Red's vise-like grip. Pat Nixon stood behind her husband watching this "red-haired fanatic"; her face an expressionless mask. Aglow with adoration, Red spoke from the corner of his mouth nearest me, "Take the damned thing!" Praying for a steady hand and clear focus, I snapped the shutter.

Once his hand was released, Nixon and his entourage made their way off stage and back up the aisle. Red had parked behind the school building and we dashed down the steps from the stage and out to our car.

"We've got to rush to the airport, otherwise we'll miss seeing them take off," Red explained. Arriving just as the Nixons were boarding their plane, we joined the people already assembled. Suddenly a figure broke from the crowd - it was Red - he ran toward the plane calling, "Good-bye, Dick! Good-bye, Dick!"

Little did he know just how prophetic this was as he waved farewell to Mr. Nixon.

Red with Pat and Dick Nixon

XIV
DON'T WAKE THE INDIANS

Our Town
   In addition to being the innkeeper, Red felt it was important to contribute in a variety of ways to the Town of Fitzwilliam.

   The Summer Recreation Program swimming lessons given at Laurel Lake caused a difficult transportation problem for the program administrators. Red suggested they use the Inn pool as long as he was free of any liability. Thenceforth, the children, properly escorted, walked to the Inn from program headquarters at Emerson School.

   The Fitzwilliam Historical Society was the beneficiary of countless foods prepared in the Inn kitchen for Strawberry Festivals and Antiques Shows. Restoration of the Blake House Museum was not started until the late 60's and, because only a few downstairs rooms were completed, a combined tour with the Inn served to enhance visitors' interest in Fitzwilliam history.

   Church Supper chairpeople sought Red's advice regarding quantities of food to order and prepare. Once, when asked how many turkeys would be needed, he quipped: "Ten, 25-pound birds; or one 250-pounder!"

   When the lead soprano in the _PTA Variety Show_ over-rehearsed and lost her voice, Red let himself be dressed in a long blonde wig and flowing gown as a stand-in. Lip-syncing the words to "I'm Only a Bird in a Gilded Cage" from a tape made by the hapless soprano while her voice was still intact, Red was the hit of the show. The sight of the conservative innkeeper now rendered *me* speechless.

There were more extensive contributions to come.

Ghosts and Goblins

In the mid-60's we hosted a Hallowe'en Parade which started a tradition for Fitzwilliam children and provided a tremendous amount of enjoyment for us and brought the town together in a way we had not anticipated.

We posted notices giving date, time and place, the costume varieties, prizes and refreshments. We had four costume categories: Most Original, Funniest, Scariest and Hallowe'eniest.

Because judging was going to be a challenge, it was decided to have teams judge each category. I contacted selectmen, clergy and business people; everyone asked was delighted to take part. We invited them to come to the Inn an hour ahead for "coffee and" while I went over their judging assignments.

Bob Berry was the parade leader, clad in an old sheet procured from Abbie, with slits cut for him to see his way. He assembled the children in the Inn parking lot where I gave the group a pep talk and told them where the judges would be stationed. I explained the parade route: down Richmond Road, once around the the common and back to the Inn, where Bob lined them up around the pool for a final once-over by the judges.

I "raided" the toy departments in Keene for games and toys; needing twelve different prizes in order to award first, second and third in each category. It was a challenge I thoroughly enjoyed.

Response to the first parade was enormous: lots of children in prize-winning costumes. The event became the talk of the town and when our second parade was announced the following year, it turned into a contest for the parents who planned and worked on costumes "behind closed doors", swearing their children to secrecy until parade day. Wonderful creations came out, including cardboard outhouses, rocket ships, dragons, a complete suit of leaves, pumpkin outfits carefully sewn and stuffed once the child was inserted, and witches with green satin high heels. The task of judging was far from easy.

Red and I loved every minute of it, especially talking to the parents as they accompanied their children through the Patio refreshment line for ice cream and cake. We were getting to know people we otherwise would never have met and they were getting to know us as well.

Bridget

The cooperative pre-school for three, four and five-year olds met in the town hall. It provided children with the opportunity to learn and grow cognitively, physically, socially and emotionally while simultaneously preparing the five-year olds to enter first grade the following year.

To assist with the school's fund raising efforts, Red offered the Inn parking lot as the venue for a country fair. He also offered our outside barbecue grill for cooking hotdogs and hamburgers. As a further magnanimous gesture, he threw in his wife to do the cooking!

It was a beautiful day. I was at my post at the grill when Red appeared with a puppy in his arms. "I guess we have a dog," he began, "She's a Yellow Lab." He told me there had been two puppies in a cage, donated for a silent auction. No one had made a bid so Red put in a slip with "50¢" on it. "Just to get things started," he explained. Then continued, "When the bidding was closed, mine was still the only one: I had a dog for 50¢! I think we should keep her."

She was already named Bridget; it suited her so we stuck with it. She adapted beautifully to our routine and spent most of her time on the Inn porch, coming inside at night and when the weather was cold.

She developed into a gentle and loving dog. She had a morning route around the neighborhood: up one side of Richmond Road and down the other, canvassing every back yard before returning to her place on the Inn porch. This would have been innocent enough except for the retrieving instinct that was an innate part of her make-up. On the "short list" of things she brought back to the Inn were a dish of peas, an unopened carton of milk, items of intimate apparel obviously stolen from the owner's clothesline still sporting their clothespins, and a dead chicken Horace Firmin, our egg man, had tossed out of the hen house.

A Very Large Rabbit

"I think you should dress up like the Easter Bunny and hide eggs for the kids to find," Red told me. At first I thought he was joking but, as he said it, a wistful smile touched his lips. "Have you ever been on an Easter Egg Hunt?" he asked. I had, but only ones _inside_ the house when I was very small; nothing as expansive as Red was proposing.

The more he described what he had once experienced, it caught my imagination and we both got into the spirit: Jelly Beans? Yes. Chocolate Eggs? Yes. Plastic Eggs that opened to hold small trinkets? Yes. There would be prizes for the most of each type of egg gathered,

and most eggs overall. The grand prize would be for the child who found the egg marked with gold stars.

We had to limit the age of the "hunters" because some children, who were not too old for the Hallowe'en event, would overpower the little ones on an egg hunt and we wanted this primarily for anyone who still believed in the Easter Bunny.

On the morning of the hunt, just in case there might be some early morning "bunny believers" peeking out their windows, I transformed myself into a large rabbit. This was easily done: I tied on a hat with rabbit ears sticking out, wore my long-johns and a white sweatshirt!

We limited the hunt to the Inn property because we did not want the children running across any roads. Still my task was considerable: I had hundreds of jelly beans and eggs to tuck in places where a small child could find them and, on the other hand, I needed an especially clever place for the grand-prize egg.

The children assembled at 10 a.m., fifty or more, each armed with a basket or bag for collecting purposes. I blew a starting whistle and "off they went!" They had 30 minutes to hunt and then gathered around the pool to count their treasures. Everyone pitched in to help: older siblings, parents, Red, waitresses and, of course, Bob Berry.

The first year the grand-prize was a live bunny, but parents asked us not to do that any more. Not having children of our own, we were unaware of how much trouble a small rabbit could be. After that, we gave a tricycle.

It was wonderful to be part of the town, and particularly the children's activities, but it only served to bring home that something was missing from our lives.

The Indians Are Sleeping

Diabetes could be inherited. "It usually skips a generation" Red would say, "but regardless of the odds for or against my passing it on, I'm not taking any chances. I wouldn't wish this disease on anyone." We had the same conversation over and over again whenever the subject of having children came up.

As a result, we telephoned the New Hampshire Department of Welfare in Keene and made some preliminary inquiries regarding adoption. A case worker came to the Inn and reviewed the state specifications and answered our questions. 1965 was half over; Red had turned 40 that March. The state recently lifted the ceiling on the age of adoptive fathers from 40 to 45 - lucky for us!

Raising a child in the Inn posed no problem according to any official requirements, but changes were needed in the configuration of rooms in our apartment. We were required to have full living quarters with a kitchen and, the case worker added, "The child must have a separate bedroom."

Our small storeroom was converted into a kitchen and Red's office became the nursery. The office equipment was moved downstairs.

In December 1966 the phone call we had been waiting for finally came. Red answered and reported excitedly, "They have a handicapped child - a boy, twenty-eight months old. The handicap is asthma." I was instantly apprehensive, but Red countered my concern with, "I'm handicapped, you know. Maybe this is God's way of taking care of this little boy." "But why not an infant?" I wondered. "Because of our ages; they want us to take an older child first," Red said, repeating what he had learned on the telephone.

By the end of the month, Joshua came to us, filling the hearts and lives of everyone, including the Mothers and Bridget. And his extended family: our staff.

The new kitchen in our apartment overlooked the side entrance of the Inn. Josh would sit in his high chair at the kitchen table eating his supper; it was dark outside except for the Inn lights. To his two-year old mind, an Inn was for "Inn-dians" and he would say, "The 'Inn-dians' are coming to go to bed. Shh! We don't wake any 'Inn-dians'."

In 1968, when Josh had been with us for a year ten-week old Amey arrived.

At night, when I said my "Now I Lay Me",
I always prayed for a sister, Amey;
And God was good: never asked, "How come ?"
Just sent her, right off, to me, Dad and Mum.
But, I never knew she'd make so much noise !
Or wouldn't know how to play with the toys.
All she does is sleep and drink milk;
But, she's ever so pretty — with skin like silk;
So, I'm really and truly awfully glad
That I did, what I did, for my Mom and Dad:
And prayed to God for a sister, Amey,
At night, when I said my "Now I Lay Me".

Joshua Enoch Fuller, Big Brother

Mary Lou and Enoch Fuller, Mom and Dad

P. S. Her name is: Amey Jordan Fuller

Born: April 3, 1968

In order to comply with state regulations that each child have a separate bedroom, we purchased the "Flagg Place", an 1840's house across from the Inn parking lot. It had stood empty for 40 years and required total restoration to make it livable.

When it was complete, Red and I, along with our two children and Bridget, moved out of the Inn and into the house we had named Stone's

Throw because of its proximity to the Inn.

Red was a proud parent and he loved the house. "Best of all," he said, "I can check on the Inn from almost every window!"

Always the innkeeper.

EPILOGUE

Enoch "Red" Fuller slipped into a diabetic coma in April 1973 and passed away the following month. He was 48.

Business at the Fitzwilliam Inn tripled during his ten year leadership. He chose _Yankee Magazine_ as his only advertising medium but greatly preferred the gratification of word-of-mouth recommendations. Unsolicited testimonials and articles appeared in _The Berkshire Traveler_, _The Mobil Guide_ and _The Boston Globe._

I continued to run the Inn with the help and encouragement of the Mothers and staff. There were many road blocks, mainly because I was untrained in the business aspect of innkeeping. To add to the immense loss of the innkeeper, Earle, the chef, had also died. Without these two thoroughly knowledgeable and competent individuals, the Inn could quickly flounder. Rather than damage the impeccable reputation Red had built, or have the operation suffer from inconsistencies, the decision was made to sell.

Charlie Wallace, a friend of Red's from their club management days, was looking for a country inn. The Wallaces became the new innkeepers in November 1973.

The Fitzwilliam Inn changed hands again in 1996 and, now in its 201st year of continual operation, is under the capable guidance of the McMahon Family.

"We offered soft beds, a good grog and fine food
In an atmosphere set for a jovial mood"